IN AN
IRISH HOUSE

IN AN IRISH HOUSE

Edited by

SYBIL CONNOLLY

PHOTOGRAPHS BY DAVID DAVISON
FOREWORD BY MOLLY KEANE

Weidenfeld and Nicolson
London

To my Mother

Acknowledgements

The editor would like to thank the following: Margaret Kennedy, Margaret Morgan, Maura Lockhart, Judy Connolly, John Connolly, James Sheridan, David Davison and Edwin Davison. Also, Joanna Edwards, Harriet Bell and Michael Dover, because their patience, understanding and enthusiasm helped make this book possible.

A special acknowledgement is due to Tiffany and Co. and West Point Pepperall, both of New York, for their generous contributions to this book.

The publishers are grateful to Nicola Wingate-Saul and Pierre Spake at the Pimlico Print Rooms, London, for supplying the prints and creating the print-room designs for the endpapers and the cartouches for each chapter opening.

The photograph of Derek Hill which appears on page 80, is published by courtesy of Dermot Donahue.

First published in Great Britain in 1988 by
George Weidenfeld & Nicolson Limited
91 Clapham High Street
London SW4 7TA

House editor Joanna Edwards
Designer Ruth Hope

Phototypeset by Keyspools Limited, Golborne, Lancashire
Colour separations by Newsele Litho Limited
Printed in Italy by Printers Srl, Trento
Bound in Italy by L.E.G.O., Vicenza

HALF-TITLE: Copper bathtub at Leixlip Castle, County Kildare
FRONTISPIECE: Dining-room table at 71 Merrion Square, Dublin, set with Tiffany dessert service designed by Sybil Connolly

CONTENTS

EDITOR'S NOTE   7

FOREWORD BY MOLLY KEANE   10

THE DUCHESS OF ABERCORN
BARONS COURT   14
County Tyrone

MRS IVAN ALLEN
BALLYMALOE   24
County Cork

MR ALFRED COCHRANE
CORKE LODGE   34
County Wicklow

SYBIL CONNOLLY
71 MERRION SQUARE   46
Dublin

LADY DUNSANY
DUNSANY CASTLE   60
County Meath

THE HON. DESMOND GUINNESS
LEIXLIP CASTLE   66
County Kildare

MR DEREK HILL
THE GLEBE   76
County Donegal

MRS CHARLES JUDD
GLENASMOLE LODGE   82
County Dublin

MRS MURRAY McDONNELL
WHITECHURCH STUD   88
County Kildare

MR HENRY McDOWELL
CELBRIDGE LODGE   94
County Kildare

MRS VINCENT O'BRIEN
BALLYDOYLE   100
County Tipperary

MRS PYERS O'CONOR-NASH
CLONALIS   108
County Roscommon

THE COUNTESS OF ROSSE
BIRR CASTLE   118
County Offaly

MR PATRICK SCOTT
BALLYNABROCKY   128
County Wicklow

MR GEORGE STACPOOLE
BALLYNACOURTY   136
County Limerick

MRS WILLIAM WATTS
THE PROVOST'S HOUSE   144
Trinity College, Dublin

DANA WYNTER
GLENMACNASS   152
County Wicklow

INDEX   158

EDITOR'S NOTE

I cannot remember a time when I was not in love with houses, beginning with a dolls' house in my childhood. In those far-off days, hours, weeks, even years were spent arranging and rearranging the rooms, moving the furniture, changing the colour schemes, allotting roles to each room, and then changing them again. A favourite pastime was to plan a schedule of housekeeping duties: Monday was the day set aside for laundry, Tuesday for ironing, Wednesday for cooking, and so on. Not just the house, the life in the house was important to me.

In an Irish House aims at telling the story of life as it is lived now, towards the end of the twentieth century, in seventeen Irish houses. The owners, sometimes the co-owners, sometimes the temporary occupants, each consented to write about their families, their houses and their lives. Who could do it better?

The late art historian, John Hunt (described by James Rorrimer, director of the Metropolitan Museum in New York, as the greatest living medievalist), used to say that food was an important part of a civilization. Because he knew more about everything than anyone I have ever known, I remembered his words and gave myself a lot of extra trouble by deciding to include some favourite family recipes from each contributor. Never having written a cookery book I hadn't realized that before publishing a recipe it has to be tested to make sure that the ingredients, timings and so on, are correct. For weeks my long-suffering family have had to endure the most unlikely combination of foods while my cook experimented with recipes as diverse as Alfred Cochrane's exotic contribution from Alice B. Toklas's luncheon dish of bass for Picasso, to the delicious simplicity of Myrtle Allen's scones. (Try eating the latter with home-made strawberry jam on a cold day in February; nothing evokes a summer's day so well.) The toffee, fudge and truffles from Clonalis are wickedly rich, and not for calorie counters.

There was a time, perhaps twenty or more years ago, when interiors of Irish houses were almost all cream, beige and brown. This predilection for drab colours used to puzzle me. Bright, sunny days are at a premium in Ireland, so surely, I would argue to myself, we more than most people should have cheerful colours indoors.

Now, all that has changed. Looking at the photographs in this book, colour is everywhere, and this makes an enormous difference to the atmosphere and character of Irish houses.

The Contributors
All the contributors to this book are hard workers. Owners of big houses and castles work almost harder than anyone I know in their efforts to keep their properties intact so that they can be handed down to the next generation. In almost all cases, they now share their homes with the outside world, either in opening these properties to the public, or allowing them to be used for special events. None complain about this situation, despite having minimal help in their endeavours.

SASHA ABERCORN, a Jung disciple, has the distinction of being a descendant of both the Tsar's family and of Alexander Pushkin, the Russian poet. With admirable calm she manages a house which covers more than an acre of ground, as well as being a wife and mother and playing the myriad of roles now required of women.

MYRTLE ALLEN is one of Ireland's best known cooks. Apart from sharing her ancient house, Ballymaloe, with guests, she writes bestselling cookery books. She radiates an incredible calm in the midst of frantic activity, which one supposes is normal for a big hotel that is constantly earning top ratings from food critics the world over.

ALFRED COCHRANE is an original in everything he does. As well as being a successful architect, he designs furniture, lamps, in fact anything one might need for the interior of one's house.

SHEILA DUNSANY, in her essay, describes a typical week in her life. It speaks for itself.

DESMOND GUINNESS works hard on his farm in Leixlip and also for the Irish Georgian Society, whose formation many years ago made us aware of our Georgian heritage and the need to preserve it. Everyone in Ireland is indebted to him for this.

DEREK HILL, painter of portraits and landscapes, is also a great traveller and writer – in fact, a true Renaissance man. Lord Gowrie, chairman of Sotheby's in London, argues that he is the best painter of Irish landscapes since Jack Yeats.

JUNE JUDD is one of the best chatelaines in Ireland. She and her husband, Charlie, love to entertain. An invitation to their luncheon held during the first week in August is eagerly sought after, and as many as ninety-five people are known to attend. They sit at tables in rooms throughout the Judd's charming house, eating wonderful food, all of which is supervised by June. She is blessed with a seemingly ageless beauty; it is difficult to imagine her being a mother, much less a grandmother of six.

PEGGY MCDONNELL, as one is aware in reading her essay, cherishes every day spent at Whitechurch Stud. She too, is an original, editing to the minimum the interiors of her houses both in the United States and Ireland. The end result succeeds in being the essence of good taste.

HENRY MCDOWELL writes so aptly about Irish life and, in his role as genealogist, can trace the history of a family, or a house, down to the last detail.

JACQUELINE O'BRIEN is the wife of one of, if not the, greatest horse trainer in the world. The day we photographed Ballydoyle was a day of memorable beauty: it was mid October, there had been a heavy frost the previous night and the sun that morning was brilliant, as only a winter sun can be. The combination of sun and frost resulted in a fine blue mist which hovered just above the ground. As we went out to the gallops, the distant mountains were half hidden in the morning mist, and in the far distance that most magnificent of ruins, the Rock of Cashel, looked for all the world like a mirage in the desert. The horses – graceful, glorious creatures that they are – began to canter down the gallops. I thought to myself, if heaven is like this, I shall be content!

MARGUERITE O'CONOR-NASH at Clonalis lives surrounded by the memorabilia of the oldest family in Europe. When at Clonalis, one longs to be able to spend a month, preferably alone, shut up in the library reading the extraordinary and unique documents and letters which form the archives.

BRENDAN AND ALISON ROSSE hardly ever stand still. A constant stream of people visit both the garden and the castle. A once-yearly exhibition of aspects of life at Birr Castle – such as the history of the garden, or the activities of a fascinating and farseeing nineteenth-century countess, Mary Rosse (who amongst other things became well-known for her pioneer work in the then comparatively new field of photography) – and an international carriage-driving event which takes place in the autumn, are just two of the occupations that fill the days at Birr Castle.

PAT SCOTT is so successful as a painter that during the first day of his last exhibition he sold every picture on show! In between exhibitions he travels extensively to far-away places, believing that living on a small island as all of us do, we need to go away, both for new inspiration and also so that we can look with a fresh eye at what is available on our own doorstep.

GEORGE AND MICHELINA STACPOOLE are involved, both equally busily, in quite different occupations. Imaginative and forever creative in her knitwear designs, Michelina manages also to be, as someone described her to me, 'the best cook in the county'. By contrast her husband buys and sells antiques and antiquarian books, and somehow, between them, they find time to organize a beautiful home and young family.

GERRY WATTS lives surrounded by another sort of beauty. The Provost's House at Trinity College is *almost* austere in its perfection. Gerry is extraordinarily generous in sharing the house with groups and individuals. Her private life must be sorely dented by the demands on her time in her role as wife of the Provost, but one is only aware of the warmth of her welcome.

DANA WYNTER lives out an idyll, having time to form relationships with the wildlife that lives around her mountain home, while all the time writing, with that irresistible combination of humour and pathos, for some of the most distinguished publications in Europe.

MOLLY KEANE kindly agreed to write the foreword to this book and we are honoured to be able to include it. No one captures the mood of the Irish country house in the earlier part of this century as Molly does.

I have dedicated this book to my Mother. In a spirit of admiration and respect I would like to extend that dedication to include all the contributors.

FOREWORD BY MOLLY KEANE

English country houses, great or small, have an air of blessed permanence. They sit low down in their wooded valleys, comfortable as cups in saucers. Most probably, the valley is crowned by a folly, usually commemorative of the Napoleonic wars. The folly stares idly down into the woods where pheasants move about, contented and well cared, while waiting for death. I can think of the house that I knew as a child, and as a teenager: it was set below just such a valley – a great bowl of cream in Bath stone, flights of steps drifting towards the river, a couple of lions to every flight. One lion had his nose chiselled away by my father, aged six. (Impossible to attribute such an act to my grave little father.)

All that is changelessly England has its embodiment, its stubborn endurance, in that kind of country house, so endowed, so superior to its Irish counterpart and, at the same time, so wanting in that quality Irish houses possess. By contrast they are ethereal in their uselessness, extravagant in the spaces their designers yielded up to one object only – beauty. And, where possible, a grandeur of spreading wings and distant pavilions. Maybe the airy elegance, the lack of opulence leaving something like a hunger for a balancing wing, or a pavilion, evident in some houses of the Georgian or early Regency periods can be attributed to the sad fact of money running out before fulfilling either the owners' ambitions, or the architects' designs.

Almost everything enduring and beautiful in Irish architecture was undertaken in the eighteenth century, to be succeeded by the Regency romantics. Only a few Queen Anne houses exist in Ireland. Before that time dwelling houses were fortified appendages to towers or castles. A tower or a ruined castle on the land gave its owner a claim to call his house Castle; for example, Castle Rackrent. Vanity, together with a certain sillyness, were rather touching characteristics of the eighteenth-century gentry. With these failings went a newly found sense of elegance, a vision to be fulfilled leaving for us so much that is ravishing, and more than worthy of the efforts made for the preservation of its still existing examples.

Sadly, Ireland today is full of beautiful ghosts haunting the distances between mountains and rivers. A house stares into a lake; not a broken windowpane, only a patient air of stupified dereliction. It is emotionally fascinating to dwell on those empty rooms where nymphs are still afloat on the plasterwork – sparse garlands exquisite in their suggestions, except where deep cracks have interrupted the amours of Venus or Diana.

I know a house where a high frieze of birds had their heads neatly shot away in orgies of after-dinner sports. When the present owner and saviour of the house had the birds' heads remodelled and restored, at vast expense, the original owners were outraged, rather than pleased, at the restoration. A legend had been defaced.

Houses have their tomorrows as well as their yesterdays. The nostalgic aura of melancholy and desolation exists – alas, with some truth – in complete contrast to the enthusiasm and determination to save and preserve much that the Ascendancy built with their hearts' blood and their great vanity, and failed, as times went through their merciless changes. It is the Georgian Society, conceived and nurtured, in their inspired youth and purpose, by Desmond and Mariga Guinness, that has been the catalyst for change, from our parents' generation of sad acceptance, to our interest and enthusiasm, and the fever to rescue and to work for so much that has so nearly gone for ever.

Another whose brain and energy have furthered the same cause is Brian de Breffny. His books, magically illustrated by George Mott, explore the smaller houses of rare quality as well as castles and mansions, past and present.

It is not only the great and important houses and monuments that have attained these promises. Obscure and often forgotten are the little, scrupulously classical, dower houses of Ireland, once married to the great estates – marriages staying undivorced through passing generations, for where else were widows and unmarried daughters to live out their allotted spans, when sons married and inherited? There were no jobs then which might support the able widow or the daughter of the Ascendancy. Their busyness, or their idleness, was housed with proper dignity. Families were responsible for their mothers and aunts and sisters, and the ladies felt no dishonour in their dependance. Members still of a court circle, the drama of every family happening held a passionate interest. They spoke to each other of the Big House they had left with absolute reverence. Its ambiance glowed behind them.

I know of two aunts who lived till their deaths in a superfluous castle, with a fairy-tale thrown in. The fairy duke, whose horse was shod all round with silver, came by rides and ways through the woods, rode across the ford at the foot of the castle and on to the forge, where the smith tightened his horse's shoes. The family fortunes were said to rise or fall with the thickness or thinness of the silver shoes.

The ladies who were housed, perhaps more cosily than their relations, in the Grace and Favours exercised for the most part a stringent and uncomplaining economy. They had their adventurous indulgences, the haunting of antique and junk shops one of their pleasures. Their precise feel for the right and charming object was an ingrown, rather than an acquired perception; the fake or the vulgar held no appeal for them. But the pieces lent or given by the Great House were not invariably of the prettiest or most useful kinds. I remember a stuffed badger that made a smelly, furry footrest underneath a buhl writing table; unaided and alone some famous terrier (property of a famous uncle) had drawn this badger from his dark sett. Now immortalized, proper family sentiment forbade his extinction. Together with his potent smell, he could be on long loan to the dower house. He was still in the family.

The creation and maintenance of their gardens was another happy and necessary obsession. I know a field of daffodils, planted by a great-great-aunt at the head of the glen where she and her sisters lived for years on almost nothing. Eighty years on, daffodils spread their magic down a hill, as far as the banks of a dark little river, grumbling and whispering low under its cover of alder and stunted oak trees. Now,

this dower house, slightly more gracious and important than any cottage orné, enjoys, with its garden, a well-preserved and well-loved old age.

Many of the great houses of Ireland, having sucked into their existence the capital of their families, are now in other hands – lately, and most fortunately, American hands. Others are still secure in the traditions and ownership of their original begetters. On some estates, the willingly dispossessed owners have resurrected and restored buildings originally intended for purposes far distant from any thought of their habitation by the descendants of the Ascendancy. Now, where circumstances have changed the ownership of the great house, the same circumstances have led to the happy reconstruction and restoration of barns, game-keepers' cottages and gate lodges. They fulfill a further and different life in the family. I know a stone-built barn, standing for many years tall and bleak as an empty church, that has become a three-storeyed house; its many windows are full of sunlight, its thick walls mature the warmth of woodburning stoves and central heating beyond the powers of any flimsy walls to maintain.

Sometimes I like to visit a true cottage orné, Swiss Cottage by the River Suir. Once it was the meeting place for glorious (hardly picnic) luncheons for the salmon fishers. Sometimes evening parties were held there, the river bank a romantic background for intrigue or flirtation. The contents of a perfect tiny cellar, complete with stone wine bins, a necessary contribution to these pleasures.

Some gate lodges have proved very worthy of conversion. Their eighteenth-century style agrees with the beautiful iron gates, once to be opened and shut at any hour of day or night by the occupant of the lodge. Carriage drivers shouted, 'Gate! Gate!' Earliest motorcars tooted their rubber horns on their way in or out of the wooded drives. Even houses comparatively near to the common highway had avenues wandering extravagantly through the estate before reaching the gravelled sweep, the porte-cochère, or the flight of steps to the hall door.

But I think my favourite piece of nostalgia is the very small and unrestored ruin of a Regency house, tucked away in the woodlands as secretly as a game-keeper's cottage. Here, with proper discretion, great-great-grandpapa kept his mistress. This little ruin is still called 'The Pheasantry'. Perhaps the name was first given as a pretext and reason for great-great-grandpapa's invariable custom of taking his walk there after church service and before luncheon, on Sunday mornings.

Turning one's mind away from the unimaginable lives of the past, it is a true happiness to acknowledge the present prosperous existence of so many of the lesser country estates and houses. I have known them in their big, unquestioning days, and I know them now when they are maintained and sustained on the work, often the manual work, of their present owners. Where their fathers hunted and shot and fished as first priorities in life, their sons get on their tractors and plough and sow and reap the lands; their farming is scientific and so is their self-educated handling of finance. Their deep affection for and pride in their inheritance is as strong a motive for work as was their forefathers' insatiable desire to build beautifully, often over-grandly. Vanity was part of the age in which they lived. And in that age, who could have foreseen how the maintenance of so much opulent beauty and style was to be obstructed and many times overthrown by changes, political and otherwise?

The immeasurable distance from those yesterdays is not commemorated so well by names forgotten and ruins deplored, as by the efforts of owners and selfless enthusiasts to preserve and maintain much that is left in Ireland for our present delight and enjoyment.

FEBRUARY 1988

MOLLY KEANE
ARDMORE
County Waterford

Opposite: *Barons Court in County Kildare is often described as one of the grandest and most beautiful neo-classical houses in Ireland. The imposing rear of the house faces south and looks over formal, terraced gardens, the lawns separated by flights of steps and embellished with balustrades and decorative urns.*

BARONS COURT

County Tyrone

I well remember packing my bags one May morning in 1966 to go and spend Whitsun in Northern Ireland. This was a country I had never visited before and I felt as if I was embarking on an adventure. I had been invited to spend the weekend at a house called Barons Court in County Tyrone – the home of the Abercorn family.

As the plane came in to land I gazed down below me at the countryside. The small fields looked like a patchwork of different greens seamed together by the darker green of hedges. James came to meet me and as we drove further and further west during the two-hour car journey to our destination, the scenery became increasingly beautiful. The Sperrin Mountains in the distance were surrounded by small farms with just the occasional white stone cottage. The roadside was edged with clusters of vivid yellow gorse.

Barons Court looked formidable at first sight, with its large portico and austere facade, but one step inside and the atmosphere was in complete contrast: warm, friendly and welcoming. Little did I realize that I had stepped inside the house that was soon to become my home and in which I would grow such deep roots.

The first eight years of my married life was divided between Barons Court where James and I lived with his parents, and a flat in London. James was at that time MP for Fermanagh and South Tyrone at Westminster, so we commuted back and forth between the constituency and Parliament, spending the holidays at Barons Court.

Towards the end of 1974 my parents-in-law decided that it was time for a change. They felt it would be a good plan for us to move into the larger portion of the house and they, in turn, would move into the wing

overlooking the lake, where we had been living. The house was to undergo a major rewiring programme, so James and I decided that we would ask a great friend of ours, David Hicks, for his professional advice in making the house workable for modern living while still retaining its classical style and elegance.

In its long history, dating back to 1790, Barons Court has adapted itself to the style of its different owners in a most accommodating and flexible way. At one stage, in the mid nineteenth century, there were fourteen children in the family and an enormous staff to run the house. Now, in the late twentieth century, life is very different and the house, somewhat reduced in size, runs on a very efficient staff of four people.

On entering the house, sheltered by a portico on the north side, you are at once in a large hall. The magnificent ceiling is decorated in Italian plasterwork of huge stars set in a geometric pattern. This great hall has no less than six doors, and I often wonder why James's grandparents, when they lived at Barons Court, made it their main living room. We often have a ping-pong table in the centre of the room and a splendid old rocking-horse resides there also. Amongst other paintings there is a fine portrait of Emma Hamilton posing as a muse by Sir Thomas Lawrence.

Following immediately out of the front hall is the rotunda. The magnificent coffered ceiling is again attributed to Italian craftsmen and is painted in three tones of grey. This room was formerly used as a music room, and Dame Nellie Melba is said to have sung here on one occasion. We now use it for large dinner parties and gatherings, and sometimes for meetings and conferences. When the room is not in use, four large portfolios of drawings by Sir Edwin Landseer sit on the table. Landseer had been a great friend of the family and it is said that he was much enamoured of Louisa, Duchess of Abercorn.

From the rotunda we move into the long gallery, aptly named as it is ninety-two feet long and has ten windows. It has a lovely south-west facing aspect and is nearly always flooded with light, even in the winter. David Hicks suggested we divide the two ends into separate sitting areas which we find works very well. I have my writing desk at the south-eastern end and, large as the room is, the proportions are so good that it is still comfortable. The major problem, I find, is that of keeping my overflowing paperwork at bay, and often I have to do hurried tidying up before the next guest arrives.

This room has seen many big occasions and celebrations. It was here that my parents-in-law, on a gloriously sunny day in February, celebrated their golden wedding with a party. We have had eightieth, fiftieth, and fortieth birthday parties, numerous christenings and even a fashion show attended by 200 people here.

There are several examples of the work of some of the finest French cabinet makers of the eighteenth century in this room. One magnificent commode bears the cipher of Marie-Antoinette and it is thought to have been in her rooms at Versailles. Constant care and attention is needed to keep the furniture in good condition as with fluctuating temperatures and the passing of time the veneer tends to deteriorate. We are very fortunate to have a great friend who is a furniture restorer. From Nettlebed, Paul Kelaart comes over to Northern Ireland about once a year with a van full

Above: *The classical symmetry of Barons Court is evident in this view of the south front. The house was begun in c. 1780 by George Steuart, and remodelled in 1791–2 by Sir John Soane. The lawns to the south and west slope away to traditional bordered and stepped gardens, with forest and lakes beyond.*

Right: *The splendid coffered dome of the rotunda, supported by Ionic columns, is attributed to eighteenth-century Italian craftsmen. Large dinner parties and sometimes conferences are held here but when the room is not in use, four portfolios of drawings and watercolour sketches by Edwin Landseer sit on the table.*

Previous page: *The front hall, with its magnificent coffered ceiling, pilasters and pediments over the doors, displays many of the preoccupations of eighteenth-century architects. Not now used as a living room, as in the past, a Victorian rocking horse sits before the chimneypiece and the room sometimes becomes a venue for table tennis.*

of equipment and works on the larger pieces that are difficult to move. On one occasion he found a box in the basement full of pieces of gilded wood. In a short while he had reassembled them into the frame of a very fine Chippendale mirror.

A favourite room of mine is the brown library. A total contrast to the long gallery it is north-east facing and dark. When we came to decorate this room David Hicks suggested using reds and dark browns as he wisely said that dark rich colours are far more warm and inviting. The entire family uses this room a great deal, and it contains every card and board game imaginable, as well as the inevitable TV and video.

A door from the library leads into the staircase hall. It is spacious in size and painted a bright lacquer red. This colour seems to bring to life the family portraits as well as a huge painting by Jordaens called *Soldiers Carousing*. We often use this room for buffet meals as it is conveniently near the kitchen and has a good stone floor. We use it for shooting lunches in the winter, children's Christmas parties and birthday parties. Tucked under the staircase there is a pianola. People of every age love pedalling away on it, sounding as though they are extremely talented pianists.

The most ambitious change we made at Barons Court when adapting the house for modern-day living was in the room we now refer to as the family room. This used to be the old dining room in the past, served by kitchens miles away in the basement. We were faced with the challenge of how to live in such a room in this day and age, as it could not be reduced in size without losing its magnificent proportions. David Hicks once again had an excellent suggestion. He proposed building free-standing units in dark green stained wood in order to make a smaller living area centred on the fireplace. The units at either end of the room contain china and glass and household needs. At one end there is a small kitchen with cooker, refrigerator and sinks. At the other end, the units house my flower-arranging equipment, and the drinks cupboard and bar. One of the windows in the centre of the room opens so that I can get out into my herb garden over a small bridge.

This is a family room in every sense of the word as the children play in all corners of it. There is a large Victorian dolls' house at one end and a hamper full of dressing-up clothes at the other end. Camps are made with cushions and rugs whenever the grown-ups are out of sight. Once I remember opening the door into the family room and seeing my godfather, the late Lord Mountbatten, poring over the cooker at the far end making fudge. Children were clustered round him and great precision and concentration was being used to get the mixture to the exact temperature required.

Barons Court, though it may be imposing and classical in design is essentially a family home. It has an amazing capacity to welcome people and seems to thrive on parties, large and small. It is an integral part of the community and numerous groups of people from far and near have been to visit the house and gardens. We have had architectural societies, the Deer Society, forestry and garden groups, and even the Georgian State Dancers from the USSR, to name but a few.

As much as I love entertaining and all the comings and goings of Barons Court, I feel it is essential to have moments of peace and stillness.

The gallery (left) has been measured at ninety-two feet, a long room by anyone's standards. David Hicks, the interior decorator, suggested its division into two separate sitting areas. With its columns and decorative plasterwork around the cornices, it is a beautiful room and at the same time comfortable and light with ten sash windows which allow both the morning and afternoon sunlight, if there is any, to pour in.

The Duchess of Abercorn is seated at her desk at the east side of the long gallery (above). The close-up picture of her desk (top) illustrates the problems that she describes of 'overflowing paperwork' and features on the right a card drawn by her daugher, Lady Sophie Hamilton.

Above and right: The brown library faces north-east and, in contrast to the long gallery, remains a dark room throughout the year. David Hicks decided not to try to introduce light, sunny tones but instead decorated the room in rich reds and dark browns. The plasterwork cornice was painted white against red to highlight the detailed eighteenth-century craftsmanship. Brass lamps were installed on tables to provide pools of light for reading and sewing, their royal blue shades echoing the deep blues in the specially made and boldly patterned carpet. The result is a beautifully cosy and inviting winter room. The family spends a lot of time here, not least because it contains a variety of games – including jigsaw puzzles, an eighteenth-century chess set and modern board games – and the inevitable TV.

A few years ago I converted the end of the stable block into what is now known as my folly. It consists of one large room which was formerly the foaling box, a small kitchen and bathroom, and high up, as if it were in the branches of the huge lime tree outside the window, a studio overlooking the lake. Here I do some counselling work, but I also have some time to myself to read, and dream.

I love to be out in the open either taking the dogs for a walk or gathering flowers for the house. I greatly enjoy arranging flowers and am lucky to find glorious varieties in the terraced borders which my mother-in-law tends most expertly. We also grow large potted plants in the greenhouse such as *sparmannia africana*, tibouchina, begonias, lilies and geraniums to fit the scale of the rooms. In the spring and early summer the magnificent display of rhododendrons and azaleas provides a wide choice of colour for flower arrangements.

Barons Court is an extremely happy house to live in and we love being able to share it with friends and visitors in large or small numbers. For they seem to appreciate, as we do, the oasis-like quality of beauty and peacefulness which, in a turbulent world, is a joy indeed.

Above: *Hector and Pushkin are here seen to be guarding the front door of Barons Court. The subtle colours of the dressed sandstone are clearly visible in this photograph of the portico with its columns, pediments and carved decoration. Situated on the north side of the house, the front entrance is approached via a long tree-lined avenue that meanders through the estate.*

Here are the recipes for one or two dishes that we enjoy. The Prawns en Cocotte can be served with melba toast or wheaten bread.

PRAWNS EN COCOTTE AMERICAINE

$\frac{1}{4}$ green pepper
$\frac{1}{4}$ red pepper
1 stick celery
$\frac{1}{4}$ cucumber
small piece garlic
5 g ($\frac{1}{4}$ oz/1 envelope) gelatine
65 ml ($2\frac{1}{2}$ fl oz) tomato juice
dash tabasco

pinch grated horseradish
150 ml (5 fl oz) home-made
    mayonnaise
225 g (8 oz) prawns or shrimps,
    chopped
40 ml ($2\frac{1}{2}$ tablespoons) lightly whipped
    double or heavy cream
$\frac{1}{2}$ large cucumber, to garnish

Serves 4–6

Chop and blanch the peppers and chop the celery and cucumber. Crush the garlic with a little salt. Dissolve the gelatine in the tomato juice over a gentle heat and add the garlic, tabasco, horseradish and mayonnaise.

Stir the prawns *or* shrimps, pepper and celery into the mayonnaise, adjust the seasoning then fold in the whipped cream. Turn into small oiled ramekin cases, cover and leave in the refrigerator to set. Turn out onto individual plates and garnish with cucumber, peeled and sliced.

Top and above: *Two views show how David Hicks converted the large dining room in the east wing into a family room. Without disturbing the yellow scagliola pilasters and half columns or the rich plasterwork ceiling, he split the room into three separate spaces using green painted wooden cupboards – which he calls 'modern island skyscrapers'. The result is an accommodating and practical room with a kitchen unit at one end, presided over by the first Marquess of Abercorn, painted by Sir Thomas Lawrence, a flower-cum-drink-cum storage space at the other and, in the centre, a family dining and breakfast room.*

This version of roast chicken is good with sauté potatoes and a mixed green salad.

JEDJAD IMER (HONEYED CHICKEN)

1 1.4–1.8 kg (3–4 lb) oven-ready chicken	*50 g (2 oz/¼ cup) butter or margarine, melted*
salt and black pepper	*65 ml (4 tablespoons) honey*
juice of 1 lemon	*large pinch freshly grated nutmeg*

Serves 6

Preheat the oven to 190° C (375° F, gas mark 5).

Wash and dry the chicken then rub it with the salt, pepper and lemon juice. In a small bowl mix the melted butter *or* margarine with the honey and the nutmeg until they are thoroughly blended. Using a pastry brush, brush the chicken several times inside and out with this mixture. Put the chicken in a roasting pan and pour the remaining honey sauce over.

Place in the oven and roast until the chicken is tender, basting frequently with the pan juices. Arrange the chicken on a serving dish and pour the pan juices over the top. Carve and serve.

There is a story that, in the mid-nineteenth century, when the Duke of Abercorn and Louisa, his wife, were staying with Edwin Landseer in a shooting lodge in Scotland, it rained every day and their chef, with time hanging heavily on his hands, became rather bored with life in the highlands. So he invented a new dish and named it Pommes Duchesse in honour of the Duchess.

POMMES DUCHESSE

450 g (1 lb) potatoes, sliced	*75 ml (3 fl oz) milk*
25 g (1 oz/2 tablespoons) butter	*1 egg yolk, beaten*
salt and pepper	*1 whole egg, beaten*

Serves 4–6

Preheat the oven to about 220° C (425° F, gas mark 7).

Steam the sliced potatoes until very tender above salted water. Mash with butter and plenty of salt and pepper. Beat in the milk until the mixture is soft enough to pipe. Stir in the beaten egg yolk. Pipe onto a buttered baking tray with a rosette nozzle. Brush with the beaten whole egg and brown in the hot oven.

BROWN BREAD ICE CREAM

100 g (4 oz/½ cup) demerara or raw sugar	*100 g (4 oz/½ cup) icing or confectioner's sugar, sieved*
150 g (5 oz/3 cups) brown breadcrumbs	*275 ml (10 fl oz) double or heavy cream*
4 eggs, separated	

Serves 6

Scatter the demerara *or* raw sugar over the breadcrumbs and caramelize them under the grill. Cool and crush them (the easiest way is to blend them at low speed in the liquidizer until crushed but not pulverized). Whisk the egg whites until stiff, then whisk in the icing *or* confectioner's sugar 1 tablespoon at a time. Whisk in the egg yolks. Beat the cream until thick enough to hang on to the whisk and fold it into the meringue along with the crushed breadcrumbs. Put in a lidded container and freeze. It can be served straight from the freezer.

Above: *The rich lacquer red of the staircase hall acts as a beautiful foil both to the eighteenth-century plasterwork and to the selection of family portraits ranged in the hall itself, up the stairs and between half columns on the landing. Sometimes used for buffet meals, shooting lunches and children's parties, the hall also houses a much-used pianola beneath the stairs.*

MRS IVAN ALLEN

BALLYMALOE

County Cork

I clearly remember my first visit to Ballymaloe. Such a big house, so cool and dark it was, after the long hot dusty drive from my home on the other side of Cork. The family, who had owned it for about one hundred years, were our friends. They consisted of Jim and Marion Simpson, their three daughters, Helen, Joan and Priscilla, and Jim's old aunts, Miss Myra and Miss Caroline Lichfield. Our visits followed a pattern. Lunch first, then a tour of the walled garden with its greenhouse and tempting fruit, an inspection of the latest clutch of chickens, and then we would go off to the beach for a swim.

Later on there were dinner parties and dances. At one of them I was placed beside a local fruit grower; I did not imagine that he was to become my husband or that the room we sat in would one day be our dining room.

After a few years of marriage my husband wanted to expand into general farming. At the same time Ballymaloe went up for auction. We thought the house and farm were much too big for us but there were no bids at the sale so, in the end, we bought it. My mother was distraught at the thought of my task in running such a big house. My husband teased her by saying, 'We'll just fill it up with children!'

I was able really to explore and discover Ballymaloe when we moved in. As a visitor one only sees bits of a house, so it wasn't until it belonged to us that I could really assess what we owned. The big entrance hall had two rooms at either side – the drawing room and the dining room – with two bedrooms the same size above them. This part of the house was built in 1803. Behind the dining and drawing rooms runs the old castle wall, like a spine through the middle of the house. It runs from the Norman

Opposite page: *On the far left of this picture, the old castle wall on the east side of Ballymaloe is just visible where it adjoins the sixteenth-century gatehouse beside the original entrance to the castle enclosure. The area became a coach yard when the house was extended in the seventeenth century and is now the route taken from the house to the farm.*

Previous page: *On Sunday afternoons a cold buffet table is prepared for the guests' Sunday evening meal. Using fresh produce from the Ballymaloe farms, a wide selection of salads, vegetable dishes and pâtés is prepared. Finally, the meats are roasted and the salmon poached so that they have just cooled by the time guests arrive in the dining room. Fresh flowering herbs from the garden decorate the dishes.*

keep at one end, round the old coach yard and down to the sixteenth-century gatehouse which originally guarded the arched entrance into the castle enclosure.

Back in the newer part of the house, beyond the dining room, was the china and glass pantry, where everything was kept safely behind a wooden grill with a locked door. Oh, I wish I had it now! Then, down a few steps, there is the hallway of the seventeenth-century house built by Lord Broghill. This hall was used for the servants to sit in; it had an open fire with a fan-bellow wheel. An early staircase built outside but joining the two houses leads out of the hall. Next to the hall was the large, low-ceilinged kitchen with a flagged floor. A big china sink with a tap, the only water supply on the ground floor, was in another room beyond.

There were no passages upstairs or downstairs; to get from one end of the house to the other, you wandered from room to room. From the main bedroom it was necessary to go through three bedrooms in one direction to reach the only bathroom in the house, or two rooms via the southern route! In all I counted fourteen upstairs rooms and ten downstairs. My first house would have fitted into one of the big rooms.

The booming prices of the post-war years had collapsed, so we found ourselves in acres of space with no money to buy furnishings. At first, when friends visited us we carried our chairs from the drawing room to the dining room and back again after dinner. At table, our voices disappeared up into the ceiling. Without the absorbancy of curtains or carpets, it was like talking at the bottom of a well. Sweeping and polishing the drawing-room floor was like navigating an ocean. I never could think which areas were swept and which were not. Cleaning down the stairs took the best part of a morning. With small children and sometimes farm hands to feed, help was essential.

However, for the first time in history, the house was warm, because we had installed central heating. My husband hates being cold. Winter dinner invitations to Ballymaloe used to mean dressing up in a kind of survival kit: for women, two woollen vests, a woollen jersey and thick cardigan, thick stockings, a long woollen skirt, and a silk scarf to 'look evening-ish'. Then we roasted in front of the fire, while our backs froze.

To create this new warmth in Ballymaloe we had to put a boiler into the lovely old dairy with its cool slated shelves. It was built into the rock under the castle wall on the north-east corner of the house. A cart track led from the doorway with its great flagged entrance step, under which Chuff the dwarf is said to be buried, down to the farmyard. Another path led down across the grass behind the cow house to a well of clear, delicious water, beside the river.

We divided the house in two and the south wing, Broghill's house, became the home of our farm manager, and later of friends and families on holiday. This necessitated all sorts of other changes. The big kitchen became their living room and we converted the glass pantry into our own kitchen. A passage was put in on the north side of the castle wall, and we no longer had the opportunity of seeing what was going on in everyone else's bedroom on our way to the bathroom. We had to change the upper part of the stairs to give access to the passage, thus shortening the landing. We finally put a bathroom on the landing as

well, to serve the south rooms where we slept with our children. All of these changes made the house more manageable, and all of them I regret. If I should ever move into a big house again, I would try to live in it in the way it was designed.

It dawned on me that I was no longer just a mother in a home, but the mistress of an institution. Mrs Simpson had always gone round with a bunch of keys hanging from her belt, and now I did the same.

With my interest in food and my growing knowledge of how to prepare it, we decided in 1964 to open the dining room as a restaurant. I was much influenced by Robert Carrier's articles on the country restaurants of France, published at that time in *The Sunday Times*. My husband loved the restaurant business and goaded me into doing more and more. I was also conscious that money was needed to keep the house together, so accommodation had to follow in order to get a licence to sell beers and spirits. Anyway, we had so many rooms; they did not deserve to be left idle.

So two years after opening a restaurant we threw the two parts of the divided house back into one and converted the bedrooms for paying guests. I gloried in having the whole building to roam around in once again and marvelled at the different worlds that exist on each side. The south is all sun and bustle with people arriving and departing. The west looks on to the wood and all the fun of the swimming pool. The north is where the birds sing undisturbed, and the east overlooks another life in the farmyard. We ourselves eventually moved to the top north-east corner of the building to a large room which the Simpsons had used for drying the washing and which we had originally made into a playroom and meeting place for the children from both sides of the house.

I had been advertising my new restaurant with these words: 'Dine in an Historic Country House!' This immediately necessitated a search in all the available local history books in case someone might say to me, 'What is the history of this house?' and find me unprepared. So in the frantic early days of establishing the business I kept my work in a sobering historical perspective by learning about my predecessors in Ballymaloe and *their* problems.

First there were the FitzGeralds, illegitimate offspring of the Knights of Kerry, who built the castle presumably during the late fifteenth or early sixteenth century and held it until 1641. They were a Protestant Loyalist family and Edmond, head of the household at the time of the Battle of Kinsale, refused to support O'Neill. After the battle, Lord Mountjoy visited Ballymaloe and knighted him. A stone bearing the FitzGerald arms is set into the back of the house to commemorate this event. Afterwards Ballymaloe became a great and affluent Norman household; members of its staff are enumerated on the pillar of the household harp – stewards, wine and beer butlers, a carpenter, tailor, cook and of course a musician. This harp was lost and damaged and subsequently found in a field; it is now in the National Museum in Dublin.

Lord Broghill took over the house after 1641 and, according to the records, built a house, a chapel, and a garden wall. There is a record of Broghill and Cromwell riding together in 1649 and discussing the unfortunate necessity of having had to behead Charles I.

Colonel Corker, a soldier in King William's army, took over the house at the turn of the century. Chuff the dwarf lived here at this time and Corker had his portrait painted and hung in the hall.

The next owner was Hugh Lumley who built the back of the house in the mid eighteenth century. The fields at the back were laid down as cider orchards and Lumley produced 'an excellent strong cider'.

The Fosters came in about 1760 and rebuilt the front with its large rooms. When they sold Ballymaloe to the Lichfields in 1835 they unfortunately gave away the portrait of Chuff the dwarf. Having read about this picture I decided to search for it. After some months of enquiries I discovered that an old lady living about twenty miles away had it in her house, but that she was very ill. Soon afterwards she died and her heirs telephoned me one day to tell me that I could collect 'the pictures'. I discovered that the portrait of Chuff was one of a pair, so both were given back to Ballymaloe after an absence of 130 years.

Now Ballymaloe is a big household again, with cooks and wine waiters, gardeners, housemaids, carpenters, family and visitors. Helen, Joan and Priscilla still come to visit us. I walk around with keys jangling, giving out stores, listening to problems, keeping the peace, teaching the young cooks and forever writing rotas and menus. At present a craft shop, farm shop, cookery school and a café in Cork have been added to our business interests. Our six children with their husbands and wives live all around, working like beavers either on these projects or in the house, on the farm, or in the original fruit farm. Some of our eighteen grandchildren are just starting to help too.

So we have dragged Ballymaloe into the twentieth century, with some regrets on my part. I am glad that the house still stands with its roof intact and the breath of life flowing through its rooms. Many people come to visit us as I once did, oblivious of all the corners and hidden places, the life and people who have lived and worked here before, the jokes and tricks, the schemes, joys and troubles of the five centuries that have passed since the Norman castle superseded the wooden stockades of the tribes.

When my children were growing up and my husband was deeply involved in farming, our pride was bound up in a beloved herd of Jersey cows. Bred for milk rather than beef, the calves had no market value. We reared them on milk and grass, fattening them as much as we could for up to about four months, and then killed them – sad but inevitable. I had to cope with the butchering of a whole animal, discovering how to cut out the best pieces for grilling or broiling and finding out how to use the rest of the meat, which is encased in tough membranes. These were very laborious to cut away before cooking. I discovered the Veal and Ham Press to be a delicious way to use this meat.

If you want to keep the press more than a day or two, do not add the fresh parsley. The veal cooking water makes an excellent stock.

Today, the front driveway leads to the nineteenth-century, south-facing wing that now houses guests. A Norman tower, part of the original Norman castle, stands to the west.

Above: *Every day, fresh flowers are arranged in each room for arriving guests. Here, hydrangeas have just been picked in the walled garden and await attention.*

Opposite: *Dishes prepared in the kitchens of the main house and the houses of the rest of the Allen family rely on the fresh vegetables and fruit grown at Ballymaloe. Some of the produce, including these winter vegetables, is especially nurtured in the extensive walled garden; other crops, such as onions, carrots and potatoes are grown and sold commercially on the two family farms.*

VEAL AND HAM PRESS

1.8 kg (4 lb) veal flank or *shoulder without bone*
2 carrots, sliced
2 onions, chopped
bouquet garni

900 g (2 lb) ham
75 g (4 heaping tablespoons) chopped parsley
2 hard-boiled eggs, optional

Serves 6–8

Put the veal in a saucepan with the vegetables and bouquet garni, cover with water and simmer until tender, for about 2 hours. At the same time cook the ham in the usual way (*ie* cover with cold water and simmer until tender, again for about 2 hours). Keep the ham warm while you deal with the veal.

Remove the veal from its saucepan, scrape and cut the good meat away from the skin and membrane, dice it and keep it warm. Now remove the skin and surplus fat from the ham, dice the meat and mix it with the veal. Mix in the parsley and the eggs, if used. Put the mixture into a bowl. Add a little of the veal cooking juices, place a saucer on top of the meat and put a weight on the saucer. Leave for a few hours; chill before serving.

Here is my oldest and most favourite dinner-party dish; I found the recipe in *House & Garden* in the fifties. It can be made a day or two in advance and cooked just before you want it.

CHICKEN PIE MASSACHUSETTS

4 broiling chickens, 900 g (2 lb) each
30 ml (2 level tablespoons) salt
5 ml (1 level teaspoon) pepper
50 g (2 oz/¼ cup) butter
4 chopped shallots
30 g (3 level tablespoons) flour
450 ml (16 fl oz) dry white wine
450 ml (16 fl oz) chicken stock

16 small onions
16 small mushrooms
225 g (8 oz/1 cup) diced, boiled salt pork
4 medium potatoes, diced
225 ml (8 fl oz) cream
450 g (1 lb) puff pastry

Serves 6–8

Preheat the oven to 190° C (375° F, gas mark 5).

Cut the chickens into 4 pieces each, season with the salt and pepper and put them into a casserole dish with some of the butter. Cook gently for a few minutes, but do not allow the chicken to brown. Remove the chicken from the pan and cook the shallots for a few minutes. Add the flour, stir till smooth, then add the wine and stock and bring to the boil. Return the chicken joints and put the dish in the oven. Cook slowly for 30 minutes, until done.

Meanwhile, sauté the onions and mushrooms in a little butter. The onions should be sweated gently for about 10 minutes. When the chicken is done, take the joints out of the dish, remove the skin and bones and put the meat into a deep porcelain pie dish with the diced pork, onions, mushrooms and potatoes.

Above: *Myrtle Allen, restaurateur, is pictured here in the pastry department of the new kitchen, recently built in the north-east corner of Ballymaloe. With a staff of fourteen supplying two restaurants (the other one is in Cork) she no longer spends so much time cooking but instead devises menus, organizes and orders the supplies and checks the work inside the kitchens. Fish soup is, however, the one dish she still insists on making herself to achieve her own subtle and individual blend of flavours.*

Right: *Splendid cooking has become a family tradition. Darina Allen, a daughter-in-law, teaches how to prepare mouth watering dishes in her cookery school at Ballymaloe.*

Cook the sauce in the casserole until it is reduced to the consistency of thick cream. Now add the cream and correct the seasoning. Pour the sauce over the chicken and cover with puff pastry.

At this stage the pie can be put aside in a refrigerator until required. It will improve as the flavours blend, for up to two days. When ready to use, brush the pastry with an egg wash and bake for about 20 to 30 minutes at 200° C (400° F, gas mark 6) until the sauce is boiling and the top browned.

The following are recipes that I particularly associate with Ballymaloe in the past. The Chocolate Carrageen was always produced for Sunday night supper and the scones at tea-time.

CHOCOLATE CARRAGEEN

10 g ($\frac{3}{8}$ oz/$\frac{3}{4}$ cup) carrageen or Irish
    moss seaweed, cleaned and well
    dried
25 g (1 oz/$\frac{1}{4}$ cup) cocoa
40 g (1$\frac{1}{2}$ oz/$\frac{1}{4}$ cup) sugar

900 ml (1$\frac{1}{2}$ pt/3$\frac{3}{4}$ cups) milk
3 ml ($\frac{1}{2}$ teaspoon) vanilla essence or
    extract or 1 vanilla pod or bean
1 egg, separated

Serves 4–6

Above: *The tapestry hanging in the main entrance hall – also the hotel's reception – is by Louis le Broquay, an artist from an Irish/French family who now lives and works in the south of France. Entitled* The Tree of Life, *it depicts the serpent and the bitten apple of the Garden of Eden in a bold modern design.*

Soak the carrageen in tepid water for 10 minutes. Put the cocoa and the sugar in a bowl and blend them with some of the milk to make a soft paste. Put the remainder of the milk in a saucepan with the vanilla pod *or* bean, if used, and the carrageen. Bring to the boil and simmer very gently for 20 minutes. Pour through a strainer into a mixing bowl.

The carrageen will now be swollen and exuding jelly. Rub all this jelly through the strainer and beat it into the milk. Add the cocoa mixture. Beat in the egg yolk and vanilla essence, if used.

Whisk the egg white stiffly and fold it in gently. It will rise to make a fluffy top. Pour into a serving bowl and chill well before eating.

SCONES

275 g (10 oz/2 cups) flour
pinch salt
10 g ($\frac{1}{4}$ heaping teaspoon) baking soda
50 g (2 oz/$\frac{1}{4}$ cup) butter
25 g (1 heaping tablespoon) sugar,
  optional

225 ml (8 fl oz) buttermilk or sour
  milk (approx.)
1 egg, beaten, optional

Makes 12 scones

Preheat the oven to 220° C (425° F, gas mark 7).

Sieve the flour, salt and soda together into a large bowl. Cut in the fat and rub in until the mixture looks like crumbs. Add the sugar and enough milk, together with the beaten egg, if used, to make a soft dough. Turn the mixture onto a floured board, lightly knead a few times, roll out and cut into 12 round 'cakes' or diamonds of about the same size. Bake in the hot oven for about 15 minutes, until risen and nicely browned.

MR ALFRED COCHRANE

CORKE
LODGE
County
Wicklow

aving been abandoned by her fiancé on the morning of her
wedding, Miss Georgina Augusta Magan left her nuptial
banquet and gown to posterity in her elegant Dublin house on
St Stephen's Green and retired to Corke Little (as Corke Lodge was then
known), her country estate near Bray. She thus became Charles Dickens'
inspiration for Miss Haversham in *Great Expectations*.

Miss Magan availed of the services of the architect in vogue, James
Shiel, to rebuild the charred ruins of an earlier mansion. In the eclectic
mood of the 1840s, a classical revival front was added to the existing
structure that was clad in gothickery on the back and side elevations. The
woodland garden was given an exotic mediterranean flavour by planting
evergreen oaks, a cork tree to simulate olive trees and yew trees as
cypresses; palms and vistas through cedar groves completed the illusion.

The neighbouring estate, Woodbrook, had originally been bought by
my great-grandfather, Sir Henry Cochrane, as a summer seaside villa a
fashionable fifteen miles south of Dublin. He was the younger son of an
illustrious if impoverished family, the main branch of which had
produced the notorious Admiral Lord Cochrane, famous for many feats
including the burning of Washington during the Napoleonic wars.

Sir Henry was made a baronet by Queen Victoria in the 1870s as a
reward for having manufactured and successfully marketed the first man-
made effervescent beverages, sold under the brand name of Cantrell and
Cochrane. His firm achieved the dizzy heights of owning in 1900 the
biggest luminous advertisement sign in the world sited in New York's
Time Square. He handed his empire on to his two sons Ernest and
Stanley, whose interests lay more in spending the money than in running
the business.

Above: *This picture illustrates the view of the house visible through trees from the driveway up to Woodbrook, the neighbouring estate. In the eclectic mood of the mid nineteenth century, a classical revival front – its peach-coloured walls framed by pilasters and anthemion acroteria – was added to the existing structure. The outlook is of a stream, fields and, beyond, the Wicklow mountains.*

Previous page and opposite page: *The front drawing room was designed as an Italianate loggia with marbelized pilasters, trompe l'oeil paintings of imaginary Mediterranean landscapes and windows overlooking hiberno-tropical flora. The contemporary furniture, including the Troy console supporting a vase and candelabra, was designed by Alfred Cochrane.*

By then Coca Cola was being manufactured; the company copied not only the idea but the bottle shape and also the original flowing script of the logo. The 'C&C' advertisement in Time Square was soon to be replaced by 'Coca Cola'.

Woodbrook, having been made extremely comfortable, was given on Sir Henry's death, to the second son, while the heir, my grandfather Sir Ernest, inherited the main seat, Baileborough Castle in distant County Cavan. Sir Ernest never liked it and was unconcerned when it burned down in 1910. He preferred to pursue a career as a playwright and marry four wives in London.

My great-uncle Stanley installed himself at Woodbrook and also had a baronetcy bestowed on him by the British monarch for entertaining the Duke of Connaught. He embarked on a career of cultural and sporting philanthropy. His residence, not really a country estate but a grand seaside villa, needed a social boost.

The adjoining estate, Corke Little, belonging to the late Miss Georgina Augusta Magan, came on the market and was incorporated into Woodbrook, forming a tidy 500 acres on the main railway line south of Dublin just outside the chic seaside resort of Bray which had been planned by the neo-classical William Dargan. Corke Little was down-graded to the status of steward's house and its farms and ancillary buildings put to the service of the villa next door. Now Sir Stanley could create his own cricket pitches and golf courses that were to host the greatest international tournaments. He even built a turkish bath for the relaxation of the visiting teams.

His other passion was opera and he seemed to have been quite an accomplished tenor. He transformed his father's indoor tennis court into an opera hall complete with raked stage, wings and scenic machinery. The Dublin glitterati would take the train that would let them off at Woodbrook station, 100 yards from the Laurel Park Opera House where Dame Nellie Melba sang twice at the height of her career and where Sir Hamilton Harty composed. So this was the inspiration for Glyndebourne.

The fortunes of Corke Lodge fluctuated with the quality of its tenants while its pretty facade remained eyecatching through the trees driving up Woodbrook's avenue. Times were good when it served as a residence for the Lords Windlesham and De Freyne. Showbiz replaced gentry in the sixties as the nearby Ardmore Studios reeled out their films. Geraldine Fitzgerald and Katherine Hepburn made it their base but later, as the woods grew closer and thicker around the little house, the standards of its inhabitants dwindled.

In 1978, fulfilling the life-long ambition of living permanently in Ireland, I gladly left behind the war-torn Middle East and, for that matter, the splendid chaotic decadence of Rome. Having finished my studies at Eton eleven years earlier, not completely transformed into an English gentleman, I had had no trouble becoming a Roman architectural student, sampling the last years of the dolce vita in a Via Margutta studio, then socializing bohemianly in a Trastevere penthouse and being a responsible businessman in Beirut. Throughout these years I was force-fed on visual stimuli: from palaces in Rome to palaces in Aleppo via

palaces in Palermo. No architect could have been more fortunate but the recipes were rich and, after a decade of byzantine and baroque, I longed for the simple elegance of Irish country-house living.

My first year-round taste of this was in the wing of Castletown House. Desmond Guinness had offered me this idyllic accommodation in Ireland's most stately home while I restored my own house. By the time I inherited Corke Lodge it had, alas, fallen into grave disrepair and any trace of Magan splendour or Hollywood glitz had faded.

A long restoration project started into which I poured all my ideas on architecture and elegant living. Miss Georgina Augusta Magan's house could not have provided better material and, with the props and lights provided by me, let me bid you to a party – or one of my productions – in the finished house . . .

Turning off the main road bordered by the stone walls and high trees of ancient estates into a thick wood, the lane-way sweeps past the stucco facade, its faded peach walls framed by classical pilasters and anthemion acroteria. Roman flares blaze on granite altars adorning the gravel forecourt as a warm glow of candles spills out from the large uncurtained windows of the two-storeyed house. This is the *overture*.

The front door opens to the cool *adagio* of blue marbled walls and a vista through blue marble pillars down a garden avenue to a ruined folly bathed in moonlight.

Coats are shed and graces donned for the *allegretto* that ensues as guests proceed to the front drawing room. The marble walls open to reveal mediterranean vistas: some real, to the tropically planted gardens, some trompe l'oeil. Striped silks and Smyrna carpets shimmer in the reflected glow of spotlit palms in giant tubs as guests lounge on *retour d'Egypte* sofas and zoomorphic stools in front of a roaring fire. Post-modern architectural furniture echoes the seventeenth-century reconstruction drawings of Rome's triumphal arches that hang over the doors.

These doors open to an *andante* through a smaller sitting room of soft green tweeds to a gothic conservatory of succulent foliage, slinky hammocks and 'recamier' chaises longues. A *scherzo* leads you to the staircase hall of blue marbled screens of columns repeated ad infinitum by mirrors and through the truncaded shafts of which meanders a bannisterless staircase.

Having run out of musical metaphors, the guests enter the dining room and also a different mood. Lit only by candles, its walls and floors, on which the architectural motifs of architraves, pillared mantelpiece and sideboard are drawn, are white as paper. The guests and their food provide the ever-changing colour. Gathered around a glass table they take over the stage. There is no dark mahogany or heavy silver to separate them but, under the clear slab, limbs and gowns undulate like algae to the movement of dishes and glasses above.

Let this rhapsodic flight land us in the back-stage areas of this house to see how the *mise-en-scène* functions. The gothic conservatory and the folly at the end of the garden are among the architectural props I added to the house. The back of Corke Lodge was gothic in style, flimsy in construction and semi-derelict. I gave it a lift by inserting the very fine cut-granite elements taken from Glendalough House, home of our late

The staircase, constructed between severed columns and without bannisters, is disguised within the context of the hall where the grid of columns is repeated ad infinitum by mirrors. A dancing faun stands at the other end of the staircase hall, his reflection adding to the dream-like atmosphere.

Above: *The dining room – with white walls and floor and a large transparent table, which was designed by Alfred Cochrane – is almost minimalist in design, in contrast with the rest of the house. The shapes of the curtainless windows and the doorways have been emphasized with a marbelized grey architrave.*

Right: *On entering the dining room the eye is brought immediately to the table as colour and light combine here to dazzling effect. The arrangement of beautiful shells and glass complements the freshness and delicacy of the food when it arrives.*

president Erskine Childers, that was being demolished by his descendants. These carved arches, shafts and pinnacles were originally designed by Daniel Robertson – famous for having set out the great Powerscourt Gardens wheeled around in a barrow. He would have a full bottle of sherry on the start of every visit; his site inspection ended when the bottle was emptied.

For the purposes of entertaining, the distribution of, and the itinerary through the rooms is as important as their furniture. By moving the stairs away from the main axis and giving them a larger hall, I created a circular movement through the rooms and a more inviting approach to the upper floor. Cross vistas through a series of doors give an illusion of space, apart from allowing those at the end of the vista to have a good look at who is coming in. But as ambiance cannot be calculated geometrically, I found the rooms dictated their own functions.

The front drawing room, often used by me to read the Sunday papers,

Above: *A game-carving table has been converted into a bar in the back sitting room and sits beneath one of a set of eighteenth-century Venetian hunting scenes.*

acts mostly as a pre-prandial drinks room for large parties or an anteroom for the more cosy back drawing room. The lower ceiling and more informal seating of the latter suits tea-time or after-dinner conversation.

The dining room, too, imposed its limits and regulations. In contrast to the rest of the house, I treated this room with an almost minimal approach. Space seemed ample and I discovered I could fit twenty seated at three small tables. I had only just got my furniture design factory going and my three tables were glass-topped prototypes when my first lunch party with such a *placement* became quite *mouvementé* as the glass tops started gliding off their steel bases – I had forgotten to secure them with vinyl pads. Luckily my guests handled the situation brilliantly. Lord and Lady Dunsany had brought their houseparty consisting of Mr and Mrs Alfred Taubman and Maria Alice De Marsillac, Eddie Plunkett's fianceé. Alfred, a qualified architect and recently owner of Sotheby's, was not going to be intimidated by moving furniture. Neither was Maria Alice, also an architect, who steered her *petite table* elegantly through the courses.

Above: *A deep green towel in the bathroom at Corke Lodge bears Alfred Cochrane's initial. The small, circular washstand and china ewer standing beside it combine with the prints on the wall to make this room cosy and old-fashioned.*

It took me a season to figure out the optimum number for the room was not more than twelve. I can now seat that number at one table and my small sitting room can comfortably accommodate so many. However much I love putting on a black tie for other people's dinners I never have been tempted to do so at my own. I do not consider my house is that grand or formal. Black-tie dinners presuppose impeccable waitering and butlers have to be booked too long in advance. So usually – but depending on the guests and the mood – we help ourselves at a small buffet. I like the first course to be on the table as we come in. In a white dining room with transparent table and candle sticks it seems important to focus on pretty and delicious-looking food. Also, I hate long intervals waiting for courses to appear. My meals can be consumed at a leisurely rate but I do like to get up and move all to the small sitting room for coffee and liqueurs.

Over the years the big house at Woodbrook had stolen all the limelight. The rare days my mother or brother are fortunate enough to be there, a select few are privileged to sample their dazzling receptions. But with the help of one person and the fact that I am in situ, I have allowed Corke Lodge occasionally to upstage Woodbrook. This one person is John Keenan who has dedicated his professional life to the running of a grand house. For as long as I can remember, John has kept my parents' house to immaculate standards. He is the perfect stage manager who, behind the scenes, organizes everything from gorgeous *centres de tables* to fresh bars of soap, tall candles and pot pourri.

Woodbrook being closed for most of the year he lavishes his talents on my parties. I have found myself having to keep from him the fact that I may have asked half a dozen friends back for spaghetti so as not to find every room ablaze with flowers and the table bedecked with silver.

My day-to-day living, however, takes place on the first floor where the library is. That is where I sit watching telly. I created a high-gothic interior to house a collection of medieval wood carvings. For this I resorted to the use of elements thrown out of the church of the Holy Redeemer in Bray during the iconoclastic frenzy of post-Vatican II.

These charming hiberno-romanesque arches designed by W. H. Byrne had been salvaged by my parents to create a chapel at Woodbrook. They were then reused by me to design a hermitage for my father in one of the cottages and, when that was no longer needed, I could not resist moving them to my own house. The library leads on to my bedroom and forms a very cosy apartment in winter.

My guest bedrooms lead off the various landings and are not decorated in the designer look of the rest of the house. Indeed my main guest room with the de rigueur Dame Laura Ashley bathroom has been named after its first guest, Madame Weygand. Neé Hume of Humewood Castle in County Wicklow, she is the daughter-in-law of the French marshal and an exquisite chatelaine. My next guest was the Hon. Mrs Aileen Plunket, a Guinness heiress and chatelaine of the fairytale Luttrellstown Castle. These two ladies, whose standards of hospitality are equalled by none, were the easiest people I have ever had to entertain. Their great knowledge of elegant living matched their faculties of appreciation of every detail John or myself had taken care off. I realized that the most

Left: *The library upstairs has been gothicized with hiberno-romanesque arches designed by W. H. Byrne and salvaged from the Church of the Holy Redeemer in Bray. The room was designed to house a collection of beautiful medieval wood carvings and the atmosphere is enhanced by ecclesiastic candlesticks, hidden niches and dark furniture.*

demanding host makes the easiest guest. They added such credibility to my entertaining that on my first all-day St Stephen's Day party, when I opened my doors to all I knew, everyone asked to be taken up to see Madame Weygand's room – that is, until the rumour went around about my bathroom, a cosy old-fashioned room with prints of unclad gods and goddesses to remind me to keep in shape.

Hanging amongst this Parnassus is a photograph of me in my twenties dressed as a satyr for a party given by the Princess of Villafranca in her baroque villa at Bagheria, sitting in foliage on a pedestal at sunset and seemingly clad only in laurel bushes and the chiaroscuro. Dublin social-ites made a bee-line for this room and I heard that as two ladies gawk-ed at the photograph, one of them wondered if I was not really quite naked. 'Of course he is,' hooted the other. 'I can see it from his smile!'

Because my brothers and sister and I spent our childhood between Beirut and Ireland, as a family we were bilingual, speaking French and English with equal ease. As a result, various aspects of French culture were of interest to us. Gertrude Stein was one of the figures in French life who appealed to me and, through reading about her, I became acquainted with the cookery of her friend and companion, Alice B. Toklas. She was an American who, early in her life, visited Paris, met Gertrude Stein and

Following page: The master bedroom was inspired by the comfortable interior of a field tent with its platform bed, rugs, 'campaign' chairs and impression of poles and a backcloth. Cupboards built into the corners of the room are intriguingly disguised by the strong colour of the backcloth and its horizontal emphasis. A medieval architectural capriccio sits on the mantelpiece.

43

remained in France until she died.

They entertained many writers and artists and one day, when Picasso was coming to luncheon, this was the fish dish that Alice B. Toklas prepared for him, told in her own words (from her cookbook published in 1954).

ALICE B. TOKLAS' BASS

I chose a fine striped bass and cooked it according to a theory of my grandmother who had no experience in cooking and who rarely saw her kitchen but who had endless theories about cooking, as well as about many other things. She contended that a fish, having lived its life in water, once caught should have no further contact with the element in which it had been born and raised. She recommended that it be roasted or poached in wine or cream or butter. I made a court-bouillon of dry white wine with whole peppers, salt, a bay leaf, a sprig of thyme, a blade of mace, an onion with a clove of garlic stuck in it, a carrot, a leek, and a bouquet of fines herbes. This was gently boiled in the fish-kettle for half-an-hour and then put aside to cool. Then the fish was placed on the rack, the fish-kettle covered and slowly brought to a boil, and the fish poached for 20 minutes. Taken from the fire it was left to cool in the court-bouillon. It was then carefully drained, dried, and placed on the fish platter. A short time before serving it I covered the fish with an ordinary mayonnaise and, using a pastry tube, decorated it with a red mayonnaise not coloured with catsup – horror of horrors – but with tomato paste. Then I made a design with sieved hard-boiled eggs, the whites and the yolks apart, with truffles and with finely chopped fines herbes. I was proud of my chef d'oeuvre when it was served and Picasso exclaimed at its beauty. 'But,' said he, 'should it not rather have been made in honour of Matisse than of me?'

Again, this recipe comes from Miss Toklas' book.

PEACHES OR NECTARINES GLACEES

Put six fine peaches or nectarines in hot water only long enough to peel. Prepare a syrup of 1 cup sugar and $\frac{3}{4}$ cup water. Poach the peaches or nectarines covered in the syrup over a low flame for four minutes. Remove peaches or nectarines and drain. When the syrup is quite thick, after about three minutes further cooking, pour over peaches or nectarines. See that it adheres. When cold, place peaches or nectarines on a serving dish in refrigerator for at least two hours. Prepare a puree of 1 lb fresh strawberries, $\frac{1}{4}$ cup icing sugar, add 2 tablespoons best brandy and 1 cup whipped cream. Put in refrigerator for at least 2 hours. Before serving pour puree over peaches or nectarines.

SYBIL CONNOLLY

71
MERRION
SQUARE
Dublin

I love my house. Of course, it was not always *my* house.

Records show that as early as 1782 no. 17 Merrion Square, as it was known then, was occupied by Judge Henn, his wife Helen, and son William. The Henns were a family who for many generations had distinguished themselves in the field of law. They were sufficiently prosperous to own a country estate – Paradise Hall – in the County of Clare. In 1760 it was described by Lloyd in his survey of that county as being 'one of the most beautiful seats in the kingdom'. With the Irish predilection for nick-names, the family were commonly referred to as 'The Henns of Paradise'.

Towards the middle of the nineteenth century, the number of the house in Merrion Square was for some reason changed from no. 17 to no. 71, and so it remains today.

Considering the house is over 200 years old, surprisingly few families have occupied it. Earlier in this century, Princess Margaret of Hesse and the Rhine, was born in what was then the day nursery, and which now is my dining room. Her father, Lord Geddes, was professor of anatomy at the Royal College of Surgeons, on St Stephen's Green, and this house was their home. On occasions her great love of music brings her back to Ireland, usually to attend the Wexford Opera Festival. Returning to the house where she was born encourages a mood of nostalgia. She recalls with affection the names of housemaids, footmen, cooks and other members of the household, who worked for her family. I like to feel she has a sense of homecoming when she is here.

Youth is a time to dream dreams, and my particular dream was to open the first couture house in Ireland. It was with this purpose in mind that in

Above: The delicate tracery in the fanlight supported by Ionic columns indicates the age of the houses in Merrion Square. The terraces were built in the centre of Dublin in the mid eighteenth century to classical proportions and surround a large landscaped garden.

Opposite page: The main bedroom is at the top of the house and commands splendid views over the garden, across the city and beyond, to the Dublin mountains. The fruitwood day-bed made in France in the early nineteenth century is perfectly placed for relaxed enjoyment of this southerly aspect.

Previous page: The dark marbelized surface of an Irish nineteenth-century side table sets off a collection of silver and ceramic pieces displayed beside a bowl of fresh fruit. The silver spoon was designed by Peter Bateman in the late eighteenth century, the sugar sifter is nineteenth-century English and the sauce boat in the form of lettuce leaves is twentieth century. A kiwi fruit and a peach sit on one of the Tiffany plates Sybil Connolly has recently designed.

1957 I saw, and subsequently bought, 71 Merrion Square. In Paris, Coco Chanel had always lived above the shop, so to speak. It did not seem incongruous for me to decide to do likewise. Friends and family, with my wellbeing in mind, were slightly apprehensive of the wisdom of this, but it is a decision I have never found cause to regret. Inspiration is a fragile and fleeting thing – one has to capture it at the moment of conception, otherwise it is gone. Living as I do, everything I need to translate inspiration into reality is within reach. Designing is a solitary occupation. One has to be inwardly attentive – a sort of listening, to be sure that the message comes through correctly. One's first vision is pure and unencumbered, but then that vision has to be disciplined into form. To do this one has to be alone.

During the early years in the house, when its five floors were being transformed into both a couture house (three floors), and a home for me (two floors), serious consideration was given to the installation of an elevator. But it became apparent that this would not be possible without interfering with the eighteenth-century architecture, something I would not agree to do. Instead, I resolved that I would never count the number of stairs one had to climb from the ground floor which houses the workroom, five floors up, to the bedroom and the library where all my design and other work is done – and I never have!

My day begins at 5.00 am. In the late spring and summer the early hours of the day are the most precious ones. I often take the breakfast tray to the window of the bedroom and admire the view of the garden and the distant mountains. This is the time of day when the early morning sun reflects on the pretty facade of the mews guest house, casting a lavender hue over the eighteenth-century rose-pink bricks.

Across the landing from the bedroom is the library. It has a northerly aspect; the light in this room, in the morning hours, has an amazing clarity, making it an ideal place to paint, to decide on colours for my couture collection, etc. The library is the room where most of the design work is done, consequently a room which could never lay claim to being neat and tidy. Files marked 'Colours', 'Flowers', 'Designs' etc, are constantly being taken from shelves which they share with an ever-increasing number of reference books. Baskets of all shapes, sizes and weaves act as files – much prettier than a filing cabinet and so useful because each can be carried from room to room.

A large willow basket, woven for me by a wonderful craftsman in Lismore, County Waterford, and originally intended for carrying flowers, fruit, and vegetables from the garden, held all the text, notes, and transparencies for the eight months that *In an Irish Garden*, the book I co-edited with Helen Dillon, was in the making.

As I write, I am looking around this room which is labelled 'library' and wondering if it has become something of a misnomer; 'studio' would be more appropriate. As well as walls of books and files, it also accommodates the paraphernalia required to facilitate the various aspects of my design career. Now that I pause to think about it, I realize that the capacious Edwardian sofa and chairs, made for my grandfather's library at the turn of the century, have not been sat upon by me for at least two years! Instead the sofa is draped with lengths of fabric sent to me to check

for colour, before they go for final printing. As a result of searching for a particular blue (it is a razor's edge between a right or a wrong colour), the contents of a file marked 'Colour' are strewn across a chair; another chair holds embryonic artwork ideas for china. On an easel in a corner of the room, is a newly completed painting of a wallpaper design. I despair of this room ever being tidy again!

But, of course, the house has a dual role to play. As well as being the headquarters of Sybil Connolly Limited, it is also my home. The two roles have coexisted comfortably together now for thirty-one years. I seem to need to be designer and housekeeper. In a way, the two aspects of my life complement each other; both roles are necessary to my wellbeing. After a day of intensive concentration on design, I tend to feel mentally exhausted. Tidying the linen cupboard, picking herbs and rose petals in the garden, spreading them out to dry in the linen cupboard – the rose petals for pot pourri, the herbs for culinary purposes – even washing dishes, all have a therapeutic effect. Household duties are conducive to quiet contemplation, a drawing together of self.

If the library is the centre of activity for designing, certainly the kitchen is that for the household. I have a cook (and a good cook she is too). If I did not, I would be inclined to live on fruit and jasmine tea. As a special treat, sometimes on a Saturday morning, with the invaluable help of James, I try out a recipe that has taken my fancy. Inevitably a household becomes known for its capability in making certain dishes. But no matter how good a dish may be, one cannot always serve the same food. For this reason, it is nice to be able to add five or six new dishes a year to one's repertoire.

Above: *The Coles wallpaper in the main bedroom was especially designed and printed to echo the delicate pattern on pieces of Angoulême china displayed on the mantelpiece. These pieces were made to commemorate the birth of the Duc d'Angoulême at Versailles; he was later to marry Marie Antoinette's daughter.*

Right: *These bedhangings and the coordinating bedlinen are printed with a cornucopia of flowers and fruit, a design that was created exclusively for Martex by Sybil Connolly.*

Top: *A small altar in the main bedroom contains a crucifix that is a copy of the fifteenth-century crucifix reputed to have spoken to St Francis of Assissi. A sixteenth-century needlework picture of the annunciation hangs on the lefthand door.*

Above: *At one end of her mews sitting room, Sybil Connolly sits at her desk before a pine bookcase displaying shells and ceramics.*

Opposite: *The early nineteenth-century marble-topped table in the main bedroom displays a collection of shells alongside a blue and white Korean water bottle and a Chinese export plate with an unusual marbelized border, both of which date from the eighteenth century. The Italian picture on the wall above is one of a pair depicting the sibyls or prophetesses.*

I enjoy arranging a luncheon or dinner-party – consulting with James about which linen, silver and china we might use. It is nice to use things which are indigenous to one's country, so the table mats are almost always made from Irish linen or Irish lace. The silver, too, is Irish, as is the glass. Usually the table decoration has a theme. If the main course is fish, as it often is in the summer when fresh salmon and Dublin Bay prawns are in good supply, we might decide on a shell theme. A pair of early Beleek fruit dishes with dolphins as their base, are filled with exotic and colourful shells, collected many years ago on the beaches of the Yasawa Islands, off the coast of Fiji. (I cruised these islands on my way back from Australia, where I had been invited to show the couture collection.) Lily of the valley is my favourite flower, and in May, when the garden is filled with its heady scent, I love to pick armfuls and arrange them in an early nineteenth-century oval-shaped Waterford glass bowl, for the centre of the dining-room table.

No piece on this house would be complete without writing something about James. James came to me about twenty-three years ago on the high recommendation of a dear friend, Lady Donoghmore. During our first interview I explained that as I lived alone, I did not need anyone as grand as a butler, so, would he be willing to do other things besides buttling? We agreed to give each other a trial and now, twenty-three years on, I can honestly say that without James I would be unable to live in this house. Apart altogether from his abilities, which are considerable, he is a nice human being. When guests stay at the mews, he cherishes them to such an extent that I suspect they return here, not so much for me, as for James!

It is my good fortune to live in a house in this virtually untouched eighteenth-century square. Looking out from the tall Georgian windows, I enjoy watching the seasons come and go. There are a few weeks in late spring when the horsechestnut trees, the lilac and laburnum, and many other flowering shrubs and trees are in full bloom. Perhaps this is when the square is at its most beautiful, a veritable feast for the eye and the spirit. Even after thirty-one years of living here, I still, on occasion, pause to admire the beauty of the proportions of the rooms.

Living in a house that is already over 200 years old, one is, I suppose, simply a custodian, and that for a comparatively short space of time. Inevitably one day, my tenure here will come to an end. My wish for my successor is that they, too, will find contentment here, as I have done. This is a happy house.

The first cook who came to work for me was just eighteen years old and without experience. Upon enquiry, I discovered that the Cordon Bleu cookery school in London offered a one-week intensive course of instruction, which was reputed to be infallible. There was a long waiting list of applicants; it took eight months for one's name to come to the top of the list. Although at first the cook had been excited about the prospect of going to London for a week, when the time approached for her

departure, she became nervous and apprehensive. Not wishing to waste the opportunity, I made a quick decision to go to London and do the course in her place.

By the end of the first day I had established myself as the dunce of the class! We had a particularly astringent teacher. After boiling the apricots in water and sugar, as per her instructions, I poured the syrup down the sink, and presented her with drained apricots. She gave me such a withering look that even now, twenty-five years later, time has not diminished the memory of it. Despite this, by the end of the week's instructions, I had learned quite a lot – including how to peel a hazelnut!

During the summer a favourite recipe is Salmon Koulibiac. We serve it with hollandaise sauce, or home-made mayonnaise. Finely sliced and peppered cucumber and a lightly dressed green salad make excellent accompaniments.

SALMON KOULIBIAC

50 g (2 oz/⅓ cup) uncooked long-grain rice

50 g (2 oz/¼ cup) butter

75 g (3 oz/½ cup) chopped spring onions or scallions

150 ml (5 fl oz) milk

30 g (1½ heaping tablespoons) tapioca

2 egg yolks

900 g (2 lb) salmon, poached

200 ml (7 fl oz) cream

65 ml (2½ fl oz) vodka

1 pinch each cumin, dill and paprika

75 g (4 heaping tablespoons) ground almonds

cayenne pepper, salt and pepper to taste

450 g (1 lb) puff pastry

1 hard-boiled egg, chopped

Serves 6

Preheat the oven to 220° C (425° F, gas mark 7).

Cook the rice in some boiling salted water. When cooked, refresh under running cold water, dry on a paper towel and set aside. Heat the butter in a saucepan, add the spring onions or scallions and cook until tender. Bring the milk to the boil, add the tapioca and stir until a smooth paste is formed. Beat one of the egg yolks and mix into the tapioca.

Flake the poached salmon into a bowl, add the onion, tapioca, cream, vodka and the dry ingredients, with the exception of the hard-boiled egg and rice, and stir until mixed. Roll the pastry out into a shape that is the same length and twice the width of a suitable ovenproof dish. Put all the rice in a strip down the centre of the pastry. Spoon on top of this half the salmon mixture, and over that the chopped hard-boiled egg. Spoon the remainder of the salmon mixture over the egg. Fold the pastry over the mixture and seal well. Decorate the pastry with pastry leaves and brush with the second egg yolk which has been lightly beaten.

Bake in the pre-heated oven for 15 minutes, then turn the oven down to 190° C (375°F, gas mark 5) and bake for a further 25 minutes. Serve immediately.

Without a doubt this next recipe is the favourite of the desserts we serve during the summer months. I can vaguely remember it being made in

Left: *The chimneypiece wall in the drawing room is decorated with Chinese export plates, dated c. 1746, and a pair of Chinese Chippendale brackets. In the centre there is a French cartel clock. The chintz covering the chairs and sofa is a Sybil Connolly design inspired by the work of the eighteenth-century Mrs Delaney and executed by Brunschwig & Fils.*

Above: *The table in a corner of the drawing room displays an unusual selection of objects including a silver-gilt chatelaine, an eighteenth-century flower painting of a white rose by Anne Vallayer Coster, a small landscape by Francis Wheatley and a porcelain pot and cover, c. 1699. The ceramic pea-pods and cluster of radishes are by Ann Gordon, a contemporary ceramicist.*

heart-shaped baskets, fashioned from what seemed to be very fine willow, when I was a child. As a consequence of several house moves, these baskets got lost. One can buy china heart-shaped moulds, with holes perforated at their base, in almost every shop which sells kitchen equipment, or alternatively use an upturned flower pot. But the shapes made from basket materials are the best because the waste liquid drips out through the fine muslin from both the sides and the bottom of the baskets. I was pleased to discover in a shop in New York one day, two baskets in the Coeur à la Creme shapes and I promptly bought them. Since then, I have not seen another.

COEUR A LA CREME WITH RASPBERRY SAUCE

100 g (4 oz/½ cup) cream cheese
75 g (3 oz/½ cup) castor or superfine sugar
pinch salt
225 g (8 oz/1 cup) cottage cheese

1 vanilla pod or bean
275 ml (10 fl oz) double or heavy cream
strawberries, to garnish

FOR THE SAUCE

1 can raspberries
25 g (1 heaping tablespoon) castor or superfine sugar
juice of half a lemon

5 g (1 heaping teaspoon) arrowroot, mixed into a paste with a little water

Serves 4–6

Line a pint-sized heart-shaped mould or basket with a double layer of the finest cheesecloth (butter muslin) that has been soaked in cold water and then wrung out. Be sure that the cheesecloth extends over the sides of the mould. Place it in the refrigerator.

With a wooden spatula, whip the cream cheese until it is light and airy. Slowly add half the sugar and the pinch of salt. Whip in the cottage cheese. Slit the vanilla pod or bean lengthwise, and scrape seeds into the cheese mixture. Mix well. In a chilled metal bowl, beat the cream until it is firm, slowly adding the remaining sugar. Lightly fold the sweetened cream into the cheese mixture and combine well. Spoon the mixture into the cloth-lined mould, folding the cheesecloth over the top. Sit the mould right side up, on a cake rack over a shallow bowl and place in the refrigerator. Let the dessert drain overnight.

To make the sauce, put the raspberries, sugar and lemon juice into a saucepan and bring to the boil. Add the mixed arrowroot to thicken. Leave to chill. The following day, unmould the pudding, peel away the cloth and place the pudding on a serving dish. Surround it with strawberries and serve it with the raspberry sauce.

Right: *At the end of the garden, the mews house has been converted into a guest house and contains a sitting room painted in apricot yellow and finished with a cornice made from scallop shells. The sofa is covered in 'Mildred', a butter-coloured chintz depicting camellias and honeysuckle designed by Sybil Connolly for Robert Allen.*

My grandmother told me that almost every man loves chocolate dessert, and this mousse has proved the rule. One dinner guest, sampling the mousse for the first time, pronounced it 'an edible sin'. It is a recipe by Shona Crawford Poole which I found in *The Times* cookery section.

CHOCOLATE MOUSSE

275 g (10 oz) plain or *semi-sweet chocolate*

425 ml (15 fl oz) double or *heavy cream, chilled*

40 ml (2⅔ tablespoons) iced water

2 large eggs plus 2 egg yolks

rum or other liqueur, to taste

Serves 6–8

Melt the chocolate over a pan of hot, but not boiling, water, and stir it smooth. Combine the chilled cream with the iced water and whip until it holds its shape. In a large bowl, whisk the eggs and yolks to a mousse. By hand this is hard work and an electric whisk really is a help in beating the eggs to a dense foam which drips from the whisk to leave a long-lasting trail. Then, working lightly with a balloon whisk, mix the chocolate into the egg mousse, followed by half the whipped cream and, when it is well incorporated, the remainder of the cream. Finally add enough liqueur to flavour the mixture. Turn the mousse into a dish and chill it for at least four hours, preferably overnight.

Above: *The kitchen is decorated with nineteenth-century blue and white Dutch tiles and a set of copper pans. The ceramic cheese-making jug in the foreground was made by Stephen Pearce, a potter from County Cork.*

Above: *A linen cupboard on an upstairs landing, papered in a bamboo-print wallpaper, is used to dry rose petals and lavender from the garden in readiness for making pot-pourri. The drying flowers serve also to scent the napkins and towels hanging in the cupboard.*

Left: *The tray-table has been laid for after-dinner coffee with coffee cups designed for Tiffany by Sybil Connolly. The floral motifs on the cups were inspired by embroidery on the court dress of Mrs Delaney. The coffee pot behind is English, c. 1770.*

POT-POURRI

There must be as many recipes for pot-pourri as there are days in the year. The one we use is derived from the original Constance Spry method given in her *Garden Notebook* (1940). When the early old-fashioned roses come into bloom, we gather them, but instead of drying them we mix the petals with coarse butcher's salt, a handful of salt to a handful of roses, and put them into screw-top jars. (We usually have enough for 10 or 12 jars.) The later roses, especially the ones whose petals are a deep crimson, such as Madame Isaac Pereire, we dry in the linen cupboard. The oils and orris root we get from G. Baldwin & Co., 173 Walworth Road, London SE17 1RW.

After 2 or 3 months, we mix together 25 g (1 oz/¼ cup) each of ground cinnamon, allspice, cloves, nutmeg and 100 g (4 oz/1 cup) powdered orris root, add the juice and finely chopped rind of 3 lemons and 15 ml (1 tablespoon) of the following liquids: oil of bergamot, oil of lavender, oil of geranium, oil of tea-rose and oil of musk rose. We mix these with some of the salted rose petals in the bottom of one of the jars. This is the nucleus of our pot-pourri.

When the rose petals have soaked up some of the liquids, we add the rest of the salted rose petals and stir them thoroughly in a large bowl. Then we pack them back in the jars, so that the whole mass becomes thoroughly impregnated with the oils. We sometimes now add, without salting, any dried rose petals. The following leaves also make excellent additions: dried verbena, sweet bay leaves cut into shreds, sweet balm, bergamot, geranium leaves, all dried and crumpled, and tonquin beans.

When the whole is complete and well mixed, we may add a glass of brandy. If the pot-pourri seems to be too moist it can be dried by adding powdered orris root; if too dry, some salt. During the time that the pot-pourri is being made, that is to say, from the time of mixing the first rose leaves with the oils until the final leaves are put in, it should be kept tightly covered.

When in use, pot-pourri is most effective if it is kept moist so, from time to time, we add brandy, lemon juice, and freshly salted petals.

LADY DUNSANY

DUNSANY CASTLE
County Meath

Norman castles have been a part of my life from childhood, and it is perhaps ironic that I still live in one, although in another country. I came of Welsh parentage. My father inherited two castles in Pembrokeshire. Manorbier, very large and romantic, overlooking the Atlantic Ocean, was in a very bad state of repair when I was a child. A great deal of it has now been restored and my younger daughter, Beatrice Plunkett is living there and continuing the work.

The second castle, Picton, was my family home. It was the only castle in South Wales to be left intact by Cromwell. This too is beautifully situated; a series of lakes lead down to Milford Haven and the garden is famous for its rhododendrons and azaleas. My childhood was very happy but strictly disciplined; I remember formal prayers, going to visit tenants, and accompanying my father to endless public occasions. I opened my first fête when I was aged twelve. Governesses and tutors came and went, but my most valuable education was in being sent to Florence to learn Italian and French, and to attend courses in history of art. These two years gave me a great love and interest in painting. On my return, I started meeting several contemporary painters, but it was through Graham Sutherland that I began to understand and appreciate modern art.

My first husband, Baron de Rutzen, was tragically killed as a young soldier in the Welsh Guards in Italy, just before the end of the Second World War. I married Randal Plunkett three years later. We moved into Dunsany Castle in County Meath in bitterly cold winter weather. There was no electricity and very little central heating. We thanked heaven for a hot bath, but the water smelt strange and, upon investigation, was found to have come from a disused quarry where a sheep had committed

suicide. Fortunately, there was another supply from an excellent well.

The castle was crammed with the various collections bought by centuries of Plunketts. As well, I had brought some favourite pieces from Wales. We decided to have a sale of what was redundant. Then my husband, with his excellent knowledge of antiques, bought a few selected items of furniture and many bronzes. For a year we were absorbed in redecorating, rearranging and updating the house.

The sheer beauty and romance of Dunsany overrode any inconveniences. I became absorbed in the history of the house, which by any standards is fascinating. The Plunketts were Vikings by origin, coming to Ireland in the tenth century, when they established themselves in north Leinster. On ancient maps this area is called Plunkett country. When the Normans arrived in Ireland, the Plunketts, aware that the Normans were going to triumph, did not join them, but married into them and also became their bishops and lawyers. In 1439, Henry VI created Sir Christopher Plunkett the first Baron Dunsany. He built a manorial church in the grounds of the castle where he and his wife, a Fitzgerald heiress, are buried in a large stone tomb with their effigies still clearly visible. Although in armour, a dog lies at his feet, indicating that he died in his bed. From 1439 the title has descended in an unbroken line. My husband is the nineteenth Baron Dunsany.

The castle has only once been taken by force, by Cromwell, but was recovered under the restoration of Charles II. Since then there have been many Plunketts who served their country well. Well loved and revered by many was St Oliver Plunkett who, as archbishop of Armagh, was hung, drawn and quartered at Tyburn in 1581 for treason.

When we went to his canonization ceremony in Rome in 1975, my husband took with him St Oliver's ring and watch, for exhibition in the Irish College in Rome. (These items are now so valuable that they repose in a vault in the bank.) The canonization was a memorable occasion. The day was damp and blustery – many cardinals and bishops lost their hats in the wind, and the ladies held tightly to their mantillas. There were so many people in attendance that they could not all fit into St Peter's, so we sat outside in the huge square. We had a private audience with the Pope, and were presented with gold medals. There were parties every night in embassies and palaces. It was truly a wonderful week of celebration.

In 1878, Sir Horace Plunkett, a son of the sixteenth baron, was one of the first senators of the Irish Free State and became known for starting the Cooperative movement in Ireland. My father-in-law was a playright, author and poet. He and his wife, Beatrice, entertained at Dunsany many of the literary figures of the day – Shaw, Yeats, Russell (A.E.), Stephens, Moore, Wells (H.G.) and Lady Gregory, to name but a few.

Coming from wind-swept Wales I was particularly entranced by the magnificent trees in the pleasure grounds at Dunsany. Also to my great joy, during my first February, literally thousands of snowdrops, aconites and leucojums appeared, followed by daffodils and wild hyacinths, all planted by my mother-in-law. The walled garden still had elderly greenhouses filled with figs, peaches and grapes. Everywhere there were gnarled apple trees reminiscent of Arthur Rackham's drawings, some covered with roses and clematis. Harold Acton, when on a visit,

Left: *The dining-room table is laid with tobacco-leaf Chinese-export porcelain, and decorated with four small vases of fresh flowers from the castle gardens. The portraits on either side of the fireplace are of Charles I and his wife Henrietta Maria, painted by Sir Anthony van Dyck. The convex mirror between them is sometimes called a 'hostess' mirror, allowing the hostess seated at table to see the entire company.*

Above: *The Viking Plunketts came to Ireland in the tenth century and, establishing themselves in North Leinster, married into the next wave of invaders, the Normans. Their stronghold at Dunsany is over 800 years old, the two solid twelfth-century towers on this side of the castle standing as testimony of this.*

Previous page: *The great cantilevered staircase was installed in the 1780s when Dunsany was transformed by the thirteenth baron from a grim fortress with arrowslits into a castle with grand rooms and fashionable gothic windows. A broad landing provides ample space for an eighteenth-century half-moon table displaying a magnificent silver candelabra and deep porcelain bowls brimming with pot-pourri.*

Top: *In 1439 Henry VI created Sir Christopher Plunkett the first Baron Dunsany. His body lies in this large stone tomb together with that of his wife, a Fitzgerald heiress. The dog at his feet indicates that he died not in battle but more peacefully in bed.*

Above: *The gothic library at Dunsany has mullioned windows with perpendicular tracery and a highly decorative ceiling of ribbed tracery forming lozenges and octagons. A series of corbels, resembling those used in ecclesiastic rib vaulting, support the ceiling. A family group by Johann Zoffany hangs over the chimneypiece.*

remarked politely, 'I do enjoy seeing a garden that is in no way contrived!' There was a four-acre garden planted with annuals in beds and the upkeep of this was obviously going to be difficult, so we planted trees and shrubs in place of the beds.

I used to be enthusiastic about large flower arrangements, but now I only do them for special occasions. We grow hundreds of bulbs in a cold greenhouse, starting with hippeastrums in April and ending with lilies like *speciosum* and *auratum* in September. Lilies seem to suit this house; sometimes they are picked for vases, sometimes they sit on the floor in large china pots. The dining room is usually decorated with six or eight small crystal bowls filled with any flowers that are in season. Even in winter it is always possible to find something in bloom. At the moment golden sternbergia look very cheerful.

Having finished making the house more comfortable, and improving various lodges and outbuildings, I felt I wanted to be more involved in the life outside the estate. My husband had been in the Corps of Guides in the Indian Army for twenty years, and had become out of touch with Irish life, but now he had a large farm to look after, at Dunsany. He was also Grand Bailiff of the Military and Hospitilier Order of St Lazarus of Jerusalem in Ireland, which is an international Order, with headquarters in Paris, concerned with the cure and control of leprosy and other charitable causes. I also joined various organizations and my main interest became the work of the Civic Institute which runs nine playgrounds and two day nurseries in the poorest areas in Dublin.

Last week was a typical week in my life. I opened an exhibition of Derek Hill's paintings in Kilkenny Castle; attended a fashion show for the Multiple Sclerosis Society in Athboy, County Meath; a coffee morning for the Society for the Prevention of Cruelty to Animals in Clonmellon; a dinner dance at the Law Society for the Order of St Lazarus; a meeting with the Tourist Board; and gave a guided tour of the castle for twenty people from Donnybrook in Dublin. Saturday was a lovely respite as we went to lunch with the Beits, at Russborough.

My father-in-law built a large panelled billiard room in 1912. As we were in dire need of a room for public occasions such as dinners, lectures, meetings and coffee mornings, the billiard room was adapted to fill this need. Once a year the Knights of Malta help us with a party for Multiple Sclerosis patients. Every Saturday during the winter months a syndicate hold a shoot at Dunsany, with a luncheon afterwards.

My husband and I have continued the tradition of entertaining the literary figures of the day, as well as exponents of the other arts. In our tenure at Dunsany we have played host to, in all, four presidents of Ireland, many government ministers, as well as various diplomats from foreign embassies. Many friends from the Continent, America and India come to stay, as well as children and grandchildren. We have hundreds of visitors every year. Groups arrive, by appointment, from all over the world, and they do seem appreciative of seeing an 800-year-old castle that is still inhabited by the family for whom it was built.

So, the house is kept very much alive, and I hope it will continue to be so in the future, as I do have a delightful stepson who has two charming small sons – and they all love Dunsany.

We often cook Dunsany Gnocchi when the family are at home. Obviously the recipe can be easily adapted for more than one person.

DUNSANY GNOCCHI

2 eggs	*a little milk*
50 g (2 oz/½ cup) grated cheese	*30 ml (2 tablespoons) double* or *heavy*
15 g/(1 tablespoon) butter	*cream, whipped*

Serves 1

Preheat the oven to about 190° C (375° F, gas mark 5).

Separate the yolks from the whites of the eggs and put the yolks in a saucepan with half the grated cheese, the butter and the milk. Stir on a warm stove until all are melted. Set aside. Whip up the egg whites until stiff and gradually add them to the mixture. Turn it into a buttered dish and bake for about 15 minutes. When just set, cut into squares very quickly. Spoon on top of the mixture the whipped cream and the rest of the grated cheese. Put the dish under the grill or broiler until the cream has melted and the top is just brown. The base should be a little runny.

GAELIC PHEASANT

25 g (1 oz/2 tablespoons) butter	*25 g (3 tablespoons) flour*
flour, to dust	*150 ml (5 fl oz) cider* or *white wine*
sliced breasts of 2 pheasants	*275 ml (10 fl oz) good stock*
50 g (2 oz/½ cup) chopped onion	*275 ml (10 fl oz) cream*
2 sticks celery, sliced	*fried apple rings, to garnish*
2 apples, cored and sliced	

Serves 4

Melt the butter in a casserole dish. Flour lightly and cook the slices of pheasant in the butter until they are golden brown. Remove them from the pan and add instead the chopped onion. Cook for 4 or 5 minutes, stir in the flour then add the cider *or* wine and the stock slowly, stirring continuously. Bring the sauce to the boil, return the meat, cover and simmer for 15 to 20 minutes. Remove the lid and continue simmering until the meat is cooked and the sauce well flavoured.

Take the pheasant slices out of the pan and arrange them on a serving dish. Strain the sauce and reheat if necessary. Whisk in the cream then pour the sauce over the meat. Serve garnished with fried apple rings.

Right, above: *In this corner of the drawing room, the white and gilt sofa beneath the large, gilt-framed mirror is George III, while the cabinet, with its intricate carving and delicate latticework, is by Chippendale.*

Right: *In a rack in the entrance hall assorted swords and a lone walking stick stand guard over a trio of rhino feet. The painting by Jack B. Yeats depicts a flower girl throwing a rose onto the spot where her lover was killed at Bachelor's Walk in Dublin in 1914.*

THE HON. DESMOND GUINNESS

LEIXLIP CASTLE
County Kildare

The castle of Leixlip is not beautiful but, like a *jolie laide*, it does have some reassuring features. It was built in the twelfth century high on a rocky promontory overlooking the junction of the Rye water with the river Liffey. Its name comes from the Danish *Lax-hlaup*, meaning 'salmon-leap' because of the famous leap a little way up the Liffey; this is now submerged by an electric power dam.

The castle is at its best at sundown when the Leixlip rooks fill the sky, circling noisily until they swoop to rest for the night in the beech trees. The massive grey limestone walls pierced by sturdy windows with pointed arches combine with the rooks to give a sombre, gothic appearance.

Indoors it is a different story. We live in comfortable family rooms around the core of the old twelfth-century stronghold which is now the front hall, while 'King John's room' above (he is reputed to have slept there) is a bedroom now. Our favourite rooms are in the round tower. They have windows of classical proportion which fill the interior with sun, if there is any, all day. The small panelled sitting room is where we spend much of our time, especially in winter, because of the wood-burning stove, of American manufacture.

From the top rooms of the castle you can see the town below. In 1958, when I bought the castle, there was neither bank nor cleaners at the front gate; now there is everything, including a delicatessen and shop selling Hawaiian take-away fries, whatever they may consist of. The village has a row of pretty houses called The Mall and a Norman church beside the Liffey. Under the aisle of the church lie the remains of Archbishop Arthur Price. It was he who bequeathed a receipt for a dark beer and the sum of £100 to his servant, my forebear Richard Guinness, and the same amount

to Richard's son, Arthur. In 1752 Richard Guinness set up his brewery on the main street of Leixlip, and seven years later Arthur bought an existing brewery in Dublin which bears his name to this day.

I sometimes think how peaceful life could be here if Leixlip had a moat and a drawbridge, which it may have had at one time. Today, there are nine models on an Irish fashion shoot for *Harpers & Queen* and I have been banished to the library to work in peace and quiet, somewhat wishing I was in the middle of it all. I remember once modelling an American blazer for a Japanese catalogue, sitting in my very own armchair while my hair was smoothed down and my tie straightened by a team of people, clucking over me in their native tongue. The reason for all the activity today is that a friend of my daughter Marina is a fashion photographer. He is about to go down to Waterford to photograph Molly Keane in her native habitat for the same shoot. He has chosen various crumbling Irish houses as backgrounds for the models, to convey the nostalgia that pervades her writing; he particularly likes houses with atmosphere that have not been over-done-up.

My son Patrick, his wife Liz and their daughter Jasmin, now eleven years old, inhabit the garden cottage at Leixlip, except that Patrick works in London now. Marina lives in the castle and has a son of five called Patrick with hair so fair it is almost white, and a baby called Violet Rose who has dark hair and sleeps peacefully in her pram all day long.

Except when strangers come, we all have lunch in the kitchen, sitting round a vast scrubbed wooden table with Eileen Byrne who does the

Far left: *When the castle was built by Norman invaders in about 1200, it consisted of a plain square defensible block. Many additions to the basic structure have been made in the intervening 800 years.*

Left: *The pedimented mantel in the hall comes from Ardgillan in County Dublin and is made of Kilkenny marble. Combined with the arms of the Gorges family of County Meath, set within, it provides a focal point in the hall and a fine setting for the fire that burns continuously through the winter months.*

Above: *At the bottom of the stairs saddles, gumboots, a garden trug and an old carriage trunk – its top curved to keep the rain from settling – are deposited in a decorative ensemble. The tassled and embroidered numner or saddle blanket is from Morocco.*

Previous page: *Jasmine is encouraged to climb the windows of the dining room. The castle's gothic windows with their intersecting Y-tracery appear to have been copied from a 1740s design by Batty Langley, whose lodge at Leixlip with a window of identical pattern survived the modernization of the 1790s.*

69

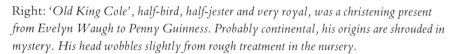

Right: *'Old King Cole', half-bird, half-jester and very royal, was a christening present from Evelyn Waugh to Penny Guinness. Probably continental, his origins are shrouded in mystery. His head wobbles slightly from rough treatment in the nursery.*

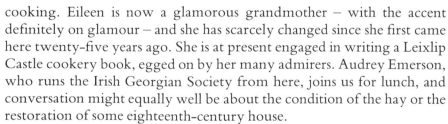

cooking. Eileen is now a glamorous grandmother – with the accent definitely on glamour – and she has scarcely changed since she first came here twenty-five years ago. She is at present engaged in writing a Leixlip Castle cookery book, egged on by her many admirers. Audrey Emerson, who runs the Irish Georgian Society from here, joins us for lunch, and conversation might equally well be about the condition of the hay or the restoration of some eighteenth-century house.

Leixlip has always been the nerve centre of the Irish Georgian Society, which is dedicated to the preservation of art and architecture in Ireland, with particular emphasis on the years 1700 to 1830. It seems incredible to me that on 21 February 1988 the society attained thirty years of age. It was born at Carton in 1958 with sixteen members, and it now has several thousand spread throughout the world.

Above left: *At one end of the dining room an early painting of the castle and village of Leixlip, by an unknown hand, is set within an elaborate carved frame from Dromoland Castle to County Clare. An entire wall is occupied by a tapestry made in Brussels in the 1680s by Leclerc depicting Caesar on his way to the battle of Brindisium and the goddess Fortuna hovering aloft.*

Top: *In front of the tapestry, a model of the obelisk at Stillorgan, County Dublin, designed by Sir Edward Lovett Pearce in 1727 as a memorial to his kinswoman, Lady Allen, sits on a black marble-topped table from Malahide Castle.*

Most of the society's funds are contributed by well-wishers, members and foundations in the United States where several local chapters have been formed. Dallas, Boston, Cleveland, Washington, New York, Oklahoma and Chicago are among the American cities where every kind of benefit has been organized over the years to help the cause of preservation in Ireland. There was even a steeplechase run on the anniversary of the first ever horse race from steeple to steeple, which happened to be run from Doneraile to Buttevant, County Cork. This was arranged at a local hunt club in Ohio by the brilliant head of our Cleveland chapter, Mrs Alfred P. McNulty.

The society is constantly on the lookout for Irish artefacts that can be reproduced to earn money for our preservation work. These celebrate

Above: *The walls of the library were decorated as a print room in 1976 by Nicola Wingate-Saul; she used French engravings to recreate this eighteenth-century fashion. Other features of the room include good mid eighteenth-century plasterwork, an unelectrified Venetian chandelier and an architectural mirror of the 1750s from the Dublin firm of Booker.*

71

the art and artefacts of Georgian Ireland by showing them to the world. We have already had some success with Scalamandré's wallpaper designs, maps, paper borders for prints and print rooms, and even furniture, the latter manufactured by the Kindel company of Grand Rapids.

Joe Price the gardener has worked at Leixlip for the thirty years since I first came here myself to live. He only works half the week here now, the other half he spends at his own Leixlip garden centre. Fortunately my wife is a keen gardener and is always hard at it whenever there is a moment to spare. She has blonde hair and green fingers; her roses are wonderful to behold in early summer. Our late-lamented housemaid, Annie Dunne, used to fill the castle with flowers. She was never known to repeat herself, nor was she ever satisfied with her creations, which are legendary. Small matter if the dusting was at times forgotten. Annie was a born pessimist. 'There's not a bit of colour in the garden' – 'Flowers are terrible scarce' – 'They won't last' – were among her favourite sayings. Nothing in the garden escaped her notice. The moment some particularly longed-for flower came out she would bear down on it with her clippers when she thought no one was looking and – off with its head! She is greatly missed by everyone.

We like to welcome people interested in Irish art and culture to Leixlip. Museum groups from the United States are quite frequent visitors; these are often subjected to a slide talk on Irish architecture given by myself in the drawing room. Sometimes new members for the Irish Georgian Society are gained in this way (sometimes, no doubt, they are lost). Visitors are generally more interested in portraits of the Mitfords than in the sporting pictures and grotesque Irish furniture that they are supposed to admire. Once I distinctly heard a very bored old lady from South Carolina muttering under her breath, 'Who *wants* antiques anyway?'

We are privileged to have been given two of Eileen's recipes as she really wants to keep them for her own book. The first, for Jerusalem Artichoke Soup, is one I would particularly recommend as being simple yet delicious.

JERUSALEM ARTICHOKE SOUP

700 g (1½ lb) Jerusalem artichokes
2 onions
40 g (1¼ oz/3 tablespoons) butter
10 g (1 level tablespoon) flour
150 ml (5 fl oz) chicken stock

600 ml (1 pt/2½ cups) milk
parsley, to taste
salt and pepper
a little cream or *yoghurt,* optional

Serves 6

Wash, peel and slice the artichokes. Peel and slice the onions. Melt the butter in a saucepan and add the artichokes and the onions. Simmer for 5 minutes, then add the flour. After a few more minutes simmering, add the liquid and cook until tender. Liquidize the soup with a sprig of

Left: *The dolls' house in the drawing room came from Newbridge, Donabate; it was probably made by the estate carpenter there in the eighteenth century. Inside there are three great empty rooms and, above child height, utilitarian shelves. Desmond Guinness has commissioned miniature copies of Irish furniture to furnish it once more.*

Top: *Built out on the south-east side of the castle into the courtyard and given its own roof, the staircase hall probably dates from about 1700. The wooden staircase itself displays hand-turned balusters of a type not often found in Ireland. The French tapestry hanging at the top of the stairs was bought by Desmond Guinness when he was at Oxford.*

Above: *In the hall a recently acquired clam shell sits on an intricately carved late seventeenth-century Irish mahogany table that came from a house in County Leix. The table is carved on both sides and designed to stand in the centre of a room rather than against a wall.*

Above: *George the gander and his two wives are pictured here strolling past the front door of the castle. The previous door was in heavy gloomy oak bearing the cypher of the Decies family who had bought the castle from Captain Conolly of Castletown in 1914. It was remodelled by Desmond Guinness to reveal the fanlight and create a brighter interior.*

parsley. Add salt and pepper and serve either hot or chilled, perhaps with a little cream or yoghurt stirred in.

SHARP LEMON MOUSSE

5 g ($\frac{1}{4}$ oz/1 envelope) gelatine
100 ml (4 fl oz/$\frac{1}{2}$ cup) hot water
3 lemons

3 eggs
100 g (4 oz/$\frac{1}{2}$ cup) castor or superfine sugar

Serves 6

Dissolve the gelatine and leave to cool. Grate the peel of 2 of the lemons and beat it into the egg yokes and sugar in a bowl. Add the juice of all 3 lemons and the cooled gelatine. Beat the egg whites until very stiff and fold into the lemon mixture. When it is all really well mixed, pour into a serving dish and leave to set for a couple of hours before eating.

Top: *This charming Portuguese statuette belonged to Lady Redesdale, grandmother of Desmond Guinness. Beside him, an early bottle of stout stands sentinel.*

Above: *Fruit and vegetables from the garden provide the family with plenty of fresh produce. Penny Guinness, a passionate gardener, returns from the vegetable garden with a laden basket.*

Opposite: *A century-old copper bathtub sits in the window of King John's room. Plumbed in and still serviceable, it bears the royal arms. This room and the hall directly below form the core of the old twelfth-century stronghold.*

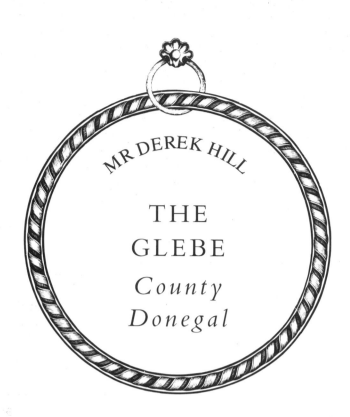

MR DEREK HILL

THE GLEBE

County Donegal

Apart from taste – and that word in itself, perhaps even more so 'good taste', has today an almost derogatory meaning – the decoration of a house is often conditioned by memories and nostalgia for the past. Certainly this was so in my case when I decorated and furnished the old Glebe House, St Columb's, in 1953 and 1954. The house was built as a glebe in 1826 and later became a small fishing hotel for gentlemen until I bought it from the last proprietor. I paid £1000 for the hotel, the twenty acres of lakeside land surrounding it and a licence to sell intoxicating liquor, which I was able to resell at once. I felt I was meant to live there having noticed, three years previously, the house's superb position surrounded by great trees and the Donegal hills on every side. It was also on a tongue of land jutting out onto the water, and I love to be near water.

The roof had to be remade and my brother John, then director of Green & Abbott, perhaps the leading London interior decorators of the thirties, suggested various interior alterations. He already had a love of William Morris designs that for long had been out of fashion and I luckily discovered a cache of original Morris wallpapers in an Edinburgh shop. I used 'Golden Lily' – actually designed by Dearle, Morris's chief pupil – for the major guests' room, and 'Blackthorn' for my upstairs study, where I covered even the ceiling. Round the staircase window I put the 'Apple' design, and I luckily managed to find curtains for the drawing room and the spare room in the Dragon Morris tapestry design. Also I bought a superb Morris carpet for the spare room and lined both sides of the study fireplace with De Morgan tiles.

Niches in the dining and the drawing rooms are lined with paper I

found in Turkish bazaars and both rooms have ornaments I brought back from the Middle East on shelves and chimney pieces. Nearly everything in the house is a memory of either places I have been to, or of friends. The French expression '*il faut meubler l'interieur de soi-même*' applies to the house as well as to myself and much of the '*meubles*' (furniture) in house, and in body, is linked with the past. Apart from the Turkish wallpapers, there are embroideries from Bokhara and Samarkand, and fans from Nara are used in the music alcove to supplement the Japanese prints hanging on a bamboo-patterned wallpaper.

In the dining room, tiles from Iznik stand beside a mosaic made in Ravenna by the firm who restored the church decorations in that city. Also, in front of the fireplace, there is a needlework screen worked by my mother. Everywhere there is pattern and design, and personal memories. A Tiffany lamp left to me by an Alabama poetess I had loved and admired, is on a sideboard given to me by my neighbour Henry McIlhenny as a housewarming present. Also on the sideboard are chianti bottles I had been given by Osbert Sitwell from his Montegufoni castle in Tuscany, with his name as owner of the white wine vineyard on the bottles. From the village carpenter of Ponte a Mensola, the village below Berenson's villa in i Tatti where I lived for five years, is a small rocking footstool that I use for books and magazines and on every wall is a picture that reminds me of painter friends – Victor Pasmore, Lawrence Gowing, Derrick Greaves, John Bratby, Edward Middleditch and, above my bed, the signed lithograph Oskar Kokoschka gave me on his eightieth birthday. The Picasso etching of an artist and his model reminds me of when his children visited me as teenagers and found the etching temporarily in the loo, hung over yet another Turkish wallpaper.

In the guest bathroom the Victorian 'loo' with its passionflower-ornamented pan given to me by Ricky Huston was a problem as the plumbing pipes of the house had to be changed to accommodate it. The plumber said, 'Mr Hill, it looks like an old ear-trumpet to me.' Then, on the electric blue hall wall hangs an original Berard fashion drawing of an orange-coloured evening coat by Schiaparelli that makes me think of the time I worked for her in Paris in the thirties, making masks for her mannequins to carry. This watercolour was given to me by Cecil Beaton who, when he stayed with me, had noted in his diary the clutter that by then the house had accumulated. The same clutter was remarked on by Greta Garbo when she came to visit and said, 'Oh Derek, for the first time in my life you make me feel quite tidy.' I would love to have painted her when she sat on the floor pouring out the tea. That unforgettable profile was outlined in the window against an evening sky.

The study where I did many of my portraits was the hotel's former annexe, across a courtyard behind the house, and is now a gallery open to the public. Yehudi Menuhin was painted there when practising for a recording session. One night during his visit to Donegal, we held a *ceilidh* (gaelic for an evening of music and dance) in the kitchen and the locals came and played their violins. My housekeeper was later asked what name the famous 'fiddler' had and, acknowledging she was bad at names, she said she thought it was 'Hewdie McMenamin'. John Betjeman, Patrick Leigh-Fermor, Osbert Lancaster, Cecil Beaton and many other

Above: *In the upstairs study, the William Morris wallpaper 'Blackthorn' decorates both the walls and the ceiling.*

Left: *The veneered table in the dining room was bought at the Smithfield market in Belfast and carried home on the back of a cattle lorry. The tiles inset in the chimneypiece are by William de Morgan. The needlework firescreen was worked by Derek Hill's mother.*

Far left: *Behind and on the lacquer and brass bedstead in the master bedroom hangs a small group of paintings including a Pasmore drawing and a Kokoschka lithograph.*

Previous page: *A Chinese cabinet contains part of Derek Hill's extensive collection of shells. Travels in the Middle East have resulted in a rich haul of decorative fabrics, wallpapers and ornaments including embroideries from Bokhara and Samarkand. The Turkish wallpaper here came from Constantinople.*

Top: *Derek Hill's discovery of a cache of original Morris wallpapers in an Edinburgh shop provided the wherewithal for the decoration of this corner, and for much of the house. 'Elmcote', designed by Dearle in 1900, provides a rich background for the obelisk, clock and boldly patterned tiles on the table.*

Above: *Cecil Beaton and Greta Garbo both remarked on the 'clutter' at the Glebe: nearly every object, every picture, is a reminder of a place visited or of a friend. Here, Derek Hill sits comfortably in his study, surrounded by books.*

friends made the journey to Ireland, enjoying the escape to the highlands of Donegal from a city existence.

So often people say, 'Don't you get lonely when you are over in Donegal?' but, remembering Emily Dickinson's letter to a friend whose sons had died, in which she wrote: 'One can never be alone with a thronged heaven above', I feel it is the same with a house. When every room and nook and cranny-cupboard is packed with a lifetime of memories one can never for an instant feel deserted or alone. Only if one's house and oneself are empty can the inevitable boredom begin and the loneliness seep in.

Here are three recipes for dishes that I love and Gracie, my cook, has adapted. The first originally came from Lady Moyne, a great friend of mine.

LADY MOYNE'S LOBSTER BISQUE

shell, claws and head of cooked lobster
6 large onions
butter and flour for a roux
1 packet tomato soup
3 ml ($\frac{1}{2}$ heaping teaspoon) paprika

pinch red pepper
dash tabasco sauce
cream and grated nutmeg, to serve, optional

Serves 6–8

Boil the remains of a lobster very slowly in water with the onions for about 3 hours then strain the liquid. Make a roux (add flour to melted butter, then mix in the stock) thus thickening the soup. Add the powdered tomato soup and paprika, red pepper and tabasco sauce to taste. Serve with cream on top, if liked, and a little grated nutmeg.

LEYLA'S TURKISH SOUP

15 g ($\frac{1}{2}$ oz/1 tablespoon) butter
40 g (3 heaping tablespoons) flour
1.2 l (2 pt/5$\frac{1}{4}$ cups) chicken stock
2 eggs
juice of 1$\frac{1}{2}$ lemons

600 ml (1 pt/2$\frac{1}{2}$ cups) creamy yoghurt
salt and pepper
a few leaves of mint, chopped, to garnish

Serves 12

Melt the butter, add the flour and simmer briefly. Slowly add the chicken stock and bring to the boil, stirring all the time. Beat up the eggs until they froth, add the strained lemon juice and beat again. Take a few tablespoons of the stock and add them slowly to the beaten eggs, then gradually add the egg mixture to the stock. Bring to the boil again. Take off the heat and stir in the yoghurt, but don't reboil. Add salt and pepper to taste and mint as a garnish.

Mona Harrison Williams was a famous beauty and a friend. Her Vacherin is superb topped with a cold chocolate sauce. As a variation, add crushed hazelnuts to the cream filling.

Above: The kitchen dresser was made locally and displays a Picasso bullfight ceramic on the top shelf and pieces of Wemyss ware together with other peasant-type pottery.

MONA HARRISON WILLIAMS' VACHERIN

4 egg whites
225 g (8 oz/1⅓ cups) castor or superfine
sugar

275 ml (10 fl oz) double or heavy
cream

Serves 4–6

Preheat the oven to 150°C (300°F, gas mark 2).

Beat the egg whites until they are stiff. Add about 100 g (4 oz/½ cup) of the sugar to the mixture and continue beating until the mixture is shining like satin. Fold in the remainder of the sugar. Spread the mixture out on two 20 cm (8 inch) circles and cook for 1 hour. Cool on a wire rack. Whip the cream and spread it over one circle before sandwiching them together.

MRS CHARLES JUDD

GLENASMOLE
LODGE
County
Dublin

O ur three-year search for a new home ended on a cold wet day in November, twenty-five years ago, as we explored a damp unfurnished house, and the surrounding 3,000 acres of land on the mountainside.

Beautifully situated at the head of Glenasmole Valley, the house had been built in 1780 by George Grierson who, in compensation for his loss of office as king's printer, had received £100,000 – a large sum of money at that time. He died in much reduced circumstances, leaving the house to his three daughters. These three ladies, following a whim of their own, turned it into a thatched Swiss chalet, surrounded by a wooden balcony. They planted twenty acres with rare rhododendrons and azaleas, the yearly flowering of which we still enjoy. Their Swiss fantasy was sadly destroyed by a fire that gutted the house to its stonework.

It was next bought by Bishop Cobbe who rebuilt it with a slate roof and renamed it Cobbes Lodge, using it as a shooting lodge. The mountains in those days, unlike now, had a plentiful supply of grouse.

Due to its strategic location, looking down the valley towards Dublin with mountainy reaches behind, it was occupied during the 1922 civil war by the IRA, which may well have saved it from a second burning, as happened to many large houses. Tommy Mahon, son of the then caretaker, tells of his mother being told to wear a large white apron when bringing provisions to the house, to avoid being mistaken and shot. The history of the Mahon family is intertwined with that of the house, as they have worked as caretakers for many generations and, happily, still do.

After six long months of negotiation we bought the property with 350 acres, which included the upper reaches of the Dodder river and its

Left: *The shrimp-coloured corridor runs along the length of one wing of the house and leads to the blue library. Plasterwork is an important feature at Glenasmole and particularly fine examples of modern gothic work in both plaster and wood are visible here above the doors. Further gothic embellishment can be seen in the ribbing of the high, tunnel-vaulted ceiling.*

Previous page: *When the Judds first moved in to Glenasmole Lodge, the house and woodwork were painted blue and cream throughout. Colour has played an important part in the redecoration of the house, and in the drawing room the cool green of the walls is warmed by rich yellow and coral fabrics, bright cushions and abundant arrangements of flowers. The painting above the fireplace, of a little girl in a red shawl with a dog, is eighteenth-century English.*

tributaries, the Cotbrook and Slade Brook rivers, from an eccentric South African millionaire. He had had the house and woodwork painted in dreary dark blue and cream throughout, although he never lived there. Changing the paintwork was, however, the least of our problems and to supervise the refurbishing we moved in with the builders, camping in an upstairs bedroom as the dust and the language flew.

There was no decorative plasterwork of any kind, and every window had been fitted with metal frames, quite out of keeping with the house. (The last one has only recently been replaced.) At the time, there was a building strike in Dublin which gave the two Maxwell brothers, of plasterwork fame, the freedom to do some very fine work resulting in wonderful cornices and architraves.

The front of the house was plain but, fortunately, we found some attractive cast-iron columns at Crowthers of London, and had a verandah built incorporating them. Even now, after twenty-five years, we are still improving and changing the house and, while it is now a lovely home, I am sure this will continue for many years to come.

When we first arrived the garden, while containing some marvellous rhododendrons and azaleas, was choked with laurel and pontigan which almost engulfed the house and blocked the wonderful views of lake and mountain. Over the years we have cleaned, tidied and replanted, rescuing, among other things, a delightful walled garden. We have opened up vistas to reveal the views of the valley and introduced many different shrubs and trees. We have also extended the garden by planting a small arboretum in what was a field, and recently added an avenue of silver birch trees from the entrance gates to the yard. As with the house, the garden is continuously evolving.

Having been brought up on a farm in Galway, I was interested in

Above: *The cool, spacious verandah, with its attractive cast-iron columns from Crowthers of London, was built onto the house by the Judds. Enclosed at one end by decorative, painted trelliswork containing two gothic arches, it is open at the front and has wonderful views across the lawn and down the valley.*

utilizing the remainder of the land productively. As a result, about 130 Cheviot sheep roam the heather-covered hills and I breed a small herd of Simmenthal cattle. These do surprisingly well on the rather poor mountainous land and, when sold at eighteen months, fetch satisfactory prices. I also keep enough hens to supply us and our children with free-range eggs, though I have to take care to protect them from foxes.

Although Glenasmole is only twelve miles from the centre of Dublin, the wildlife is a constant source of joy – and sometimes irritation – to us. Apart from foxes, wild deer are driven down from the hills to shelter in the winter and, while delightful to see, they can do a lot of damage in a garden. Rabbits abound, and I have become a crack shot with my rifle from the upstairs windows. Our greatest pleasures are the birds and, best of all, a small but growing colony of red squirrels who are now so tame they would come into the house if allowed. They are supported through the cold winters by bags of nuts hung outside windows, and are so lovely that the food that is a necessity in winter is now provided throughout the year. We must have the best-fed red squirrels in Ireland.

Aside from the house and garden, our other hobby is entertaining. While there is a constant stream of children and grandchildren throughout the year, we also regularly entertain friends in the long bay-windowed dining room, looking out over the lake down the valley. It is a marvellous room for luncheons, with the lake reflecting an unreal greenish tinge back into the sky, and with the twisted pine trees etched against the same sky, in the foreground.

At Christmas our three married children and our grandchildren – twelve in all – come to stay which is great fun and we enjoy it thoroughly. Houses love to be entertained in, and it remains one of our greatest pleasures to continue to use Glenasmole for this purpose.

Above: *At Christmas the large alcove in the drawing room is cleared to make way for the tree. The curtains, in a heavy, cream corded silk, are a perfect backdrop. The house is always full at this time of the year, when the Judds' children and grandchildren arrive for the holiday.*

For about twelve years we have given a luncheon party on the Sunday after the Dublin Horse Show. Tables are spread throughout the main reception rooms. The meal consists always of a buffet of fish – prawns, lobster, crab, bream, turbot and gravallax. This is a Scandinavian dish I discovered and for which I have become well known. I marinate raw salmon in dill and salt for two days under pressure, and serve it with a mustard and dill sauce. Here is one of the prawn recipes I use, scaled down from 'function' to 'family' size.

DUBLIN BAY PRAWNS AND EGGS

1 dozen hard-boiled eggs
100 g (4 oz / ½ cup) butter
1 dozen prawns or shrimps
275 ml (10 fl oz) cream

a little chopped parsley
75 g (3 oz) Cheddar or other hard cheese, grated

Serves 6

Preheat the oven to 190°C (375°F, gas mark 5).

Grate the eggs and beat the butter until it is creamy. Put all the ingredients into a casserole dish with the grated cheese on top and bake for 20 minutes.

Below: *In the eighteenth century, the twenty-acre garden of Glenasmole Lodge was planted with rare rhododendrons and azaleas, the yearly flowering of which is still enjoyed today. Over the years the Judds have tidied and replanted, opening up vistas of the valley, lake and surrounding mountains through the shrubs and trees.*

Left: *The main staircase has white, painted bannisters and a pale, polished wooden bannister-rail; throughout Glenasmole, contrasts of colour and texture are achieved with paint, woodwork and plaster. The pale apricot of the walls above the stairs provides a subtle, complementary background for the assortment of family portraits and landscapes.*

Right, above: *A small table in the library displays an informal collection of objects: a cluster of loosely arranged garden flowers stands beside framed family photographs, an assortment of letter-writing materials, and a pair of ash trays which are amusing reproductions of Irish daily newspapers.*

Right, below: *With fluted faux columns flanking the shelves, the library contains a fine collection of eighteenth- and nineteenth-century leather-bound books. The sofa, piled with small, square satin cushions, is an extension of the blue-and-yellow theme.*

Right: *The library is a beautifully proportioned room with an elegant Venetian window at one end. Bold contrasts of colour are achieved by the use of Wedgwood blue, white and yellow, highlighting the strong neo-classical features of the room. The painting above the fireplace is eighteenth century, of the school of Vernet.*

This pudding is particularly good for family celebrations and Christmas.

CHAMPAGNE CHARLIE

175 g (6 oz/1 cup) castor or *superfine sugar*
150 ml (5 fl oz) water
rind of 1 orange
juice of 2 oranges and 2 lemons

600 ml (1 pt/2½ cups) chilled *champagne*
600 ml (1 pt/2½ cups) double or *heavy cream, whipped*
60–75 ml (4–5 tablespoons) brandy
6 ratafia biscuits or *ladyfingers*

Serves 6

Put the sugar in a pan with the water. Boil rapidly for 6 minutes to make a syrup. Grate into it the orange rind and add the juice of the fruit. Cool. Stir in the chilled champagne. Freeze for 1½ to 2 hours until just frozen around the edges. Take out and whip until smooth. Fold in the whipped double *or* heavy cream and 30 ml (2 tablespoons) of the brandy. Freeze for about 3 hours. Soak a ratafia biscuit in each champagne glass with a little of the remaining brandy. Scoop the ice cream into the glasses and pour 5 ml (1 teaspoon) of brandy over each portion.

How we love our Irish home!

We bought the stud farm in 1968. For some years afterwards, the horses were the top priority and the house languished untouched, at the bottom of the list. Finally, in 1974, we began its restoration.

At first, I would stand outside or walk around the house, looking at it and wondering how and where to begin. One day as I was standing looking at the facade, a friend who was with me remarked, 'This house will never smile until the windows are enlarged.' She was right, and enlarging the windows was the first job we undertook. Then, encouraged by having made a beginning, we added French windows in the drawing room and the master bedroom. The house then did indeed begin to smile.

As the work progressed it became apparent that the house was perfectly suited for eight people to live in. It has a compact symmetry. Its scale, while not precisely modest, is unpretentious in the best sense of the word, inviting intimacy rather than formality. I felt we should only acquire enough things to meet our minimum requirements, so we bought eight of everything – beds, plates, glasses, etc. It was quite a shock when we arrived from America for our inaugural visit in June 1975 with all our children, plus a few extra children in tow, to find that our numbers added up to fourteen! The house was gracious enough to embrace us all.

Unlike our home in the United States, Straffan is completely uncluttered. In fact, it is so simple and spare that every time we arrive home, I step through the front door and I am convinced we have been robbed in our absence. But by the following morning I am wondering why we would – how we could – ever live in any other way.

The hall is very welcoming and spacious, the walls painted a warm 'Bahama coral'. Throughout the house the floors in every room are painted. In the drawing room the painter (rumour has it that this painter paints the yellow traffic lines down the middle of the roads during the weekdays, keeping his 'fancy' work for weekends) marbelized the floor in a fashion at once wildly inventive and subtle. Though the furniture in all the bedrooms is basically the same, made by The Workshops of the Blind, the bedroom walls have been treated very differently. One has panels of fabric bordered by bamboo. Another has a paper border running vertically from floor to ceiling creating a striped effect, the third has white panels outlined in a blue wash and the fourth is painted a warm biscuit colour as it has a northerly aspect.

Above: *The bedrooms in the house have all been treated very differently. Here, the white panels of the walls and wardrobe have been outlined in a blue wash, while the French doors, which were added by the McDonnells when all the windows were enlarged in 1974, allow sunlight to stream in across the floorboards.*

Previous page: *The hall, with its rich 'Bahama coral' walls and early nineteenth-century pine dresser, is warm and welcoming. The large papier-maché cockerel, nestling in an Irish handwoven basket, is by Mai Watts. The holes, however, were added later by a Whitechurch mouse.*

Above: *A collection of objects in one corner of the hall includes a pair of shining, nineteenth-century milk churns, a variety of walking sticks and a basket from Katmandu.*

Below: *Peggy McDonnell spends some of her time in her Irish house tending her plants on the terrace at the front. Rosemary, lavender, broom, santolina and daphne grow in abundance between the flagstones, creating a profusion of colours and heady scents.*

Right: *The wide, arched entrance door, with its white paintwork and elegant traceried fanlight, is guarded by the family dogs, here reclining peacefully on the steps.*

We have a small collection of Irish contemporary art. The latest addition (a birthday present) is Patrick Scott's *Poppy Field*. In the dining room, which is painted grey/brown with magnolia, there are Patrick Hickey lithographs, one of lemons, one of garlic, another of eggs in a basket. The door of the hatch into the kitchen is also a Patrick Hickey original. A Martin Gale pig enlivens the kitchen. There are watercolours by Michael Healy and a small bronze bull by the sculptor, John Behan.

The landscaping at Straffan echoes the same uncluttered spare feeling as the interior. There are two very old Irish yews standing sentinel in front of the house. We planted three hedges, one *leylandii*, one beech and one of *rosa rugosa*, alternating 'Roseraie de l'Hay' (crimson) and 'Blanc Double de Coubert' (white). We also planted a few trees and shrubs especially for their spring blooms and autumn colours because those are the seasons we usually spend at Straffan. Our only garden is among the flagstones on the front terrace. Rosemary, lavender, broom, santolina, daphne and blue poppies have taken over in wild profusion. What started a few years ago looking neat and organized has now become a tangle of colours and delicious scents.

We enjoy having house guests at all times of the year but most especially for the Irish Derby in June and the yearling sales at Goff's in October. The day starts early with breakfast in the kitchen – Almerinda's piping-hot scones spread with Lana's gooseberry jam all served on Shanagarry pottery by Philip Pearce, and orange juice in handblown glass by his son, Simon. Then those interested head off to the Curragh to watch the horses train. The remaining guests might like to see one of the many gardens nearby or go shopping in Dublin.

Naturally guests ask what clothes they should bring to wear and what to expect from the capricious Irish weather. What can one answer to those questions? During our last visit, the day dawned with bright sunshine but by 10.00 am it was raining heavily, then soon after a most brilliant double rainbow appeared, arching over the front gallop. Later, a softer rain fell and that night a full moon rose in a cloudless sky!

We cherish the differences between our American and Irish lives – the uncluttered house, the quiet Irish summer nights and the muffled hoof beats that awaken us each morning. Once I get to Straffan I wonder why I ever leave it.

When we have guests I enjoy giving big lunches in the dining room. They often build up a good appetite after a morning in the open air watching the training, so lunch usually involves three courses, perhaps Parsnip and Carrot Soup, a salad of cold leeks, broccoli, tomatoes and Dublin Bay prawns, with Bewley's wholemeal brown bread and farmhouse butter, followed by a blackcurrant mousse and Irish Rice Pudding. I have given recipes for two of these dishes.

PARSNIP AND CARROT SOUP

50 g (2 oz/¼ cup) unsalted butter
250 g (5 oz/2 cups) finely chopped
*   onion*
6 carrots, peeled and sliced

6 parsnips, peeled and sliced
900 ml (1½ pt) vegetable stock
salt and pepper, to taste
parsley, to garnish

Serves 4–6

Melt the butter in a saucepan, add the onions, cover and cook over a low heat until tender and lightly coloured, for about 25 minutes. Add the carrots, parsnips and stock and bring to the boil. Reduce the heat, cover and simmer until the carrots and parsnips are tender. Purée the soup in a food processor or liquidizer, return it to the saucepan and add salt and pepper. Garnish with parsley and serve.

IRISH RICE PUDDING

100 g (4 oz/½ cup) pudding rice
1.8 l (3 pt) milk
175 g (6 oz/1 cup) sugar
pinch salt

lemon peel
5 g (1 level teaspoon) cinnamon, to
*   garnish*

Serves 6

Cover the pudding rice with boiling water and cook until it opens and the water is absorbed. Heat the milk. Add half the milk to the rice and cook over a low heat, covered. Add the sugar and the pinch of salt. Add the rest of the milk and cook for 1½ to 2 hours or until it is the right consistency. Add a large piece of lemon peel for the last five minutes, remove the lemon peel, put into a serving dish and dust with cinnamon.

Far left, above: *Guests are frequently treated to large lunches in the dining room, which is cool and elegant with its high ceiling and faux panelling in magnolia and a toffee brown. The pottery on the table is by Stephen Pearce, while the glasses are all hand-blown by Simon Pearce.*

Left, above: *Patrick Hickey's lithographs line the walls of the dining room. The basket of fruit and dishes placed on this side table echo the shapes and colours of the lithograph above. The glass candlesticks, like the glasses on the dining-room table, are by Simon Pearce.*

Left, below: *A morning spent in the open air watching the horses train gives guests a good appetite, and the kitchen contains baskets of fresh vegetables ready for preparation. The painting of the pig is by Martin Gale and the bronze bull by John Behan.*

Far left, below: *The eighteenth-century atmosphere of the spacious drawing room is emphasized by two long basket-arch niches and a large mirror above the mantelpiece. A heavily fringed rug lies in front of the hearth, blending with the subtle tones of the recently marbelized floor.*

MR HENRY McDOWELL

CELBRIDGE LODGE

County Kildare

In my youth, on an Irish farm, I longed for the bright lights and to escape from the loneliness of thinning turnips in a ten-acre field. In early middle age, my dreams were of returning to Ireland to write and work as a genealogist. We decided to spend the summer of 1963 house-hunting. Our London nanny, who had once had a bad experience in an Irish castle, gave in her notice which was just as well, because the house we rented was haunted. It lay in a hollow and when it rained, the sloping lawns and the dripping ilex trees seemed to come into the rooms. I met a racing man who told me he was scared when he stayed there. 'Have you heard the fellow with the big boots on the staircase, yet?'

Each day we went to look at places for sale, motoring for miles in an open Hillman down little roads between banks of cow parsley. There was one house I fell in love with, where the staircase 'flew' across a Venetian window with a view of gorse-covered slopes and blue hills beyond. Driving away, across a valley, the car was caught in a freak wind and almost ended up in a bog. 'What *would* it be like in winter?' my wife wanted to know. 'How would the children get to school? How would the doctor get to us?'

Another enchanting place was a sham castle that reeked of every kind of rot. 'Don't-you-love-the-smell-of-old-apples?' intoned the owner, slyly watching us through narrowed eyes.

One day I came across a fox-hunting clergyman of the Church of Ireland, named Canon Brandon. He told me that Lord Carew, who was leaving Castletown in County Kildare, had kindly given a site for a new rectory and the old one would be for sale. 'Come and see it,' invited the canon, and as we drove through the gates Joan declared that this was

94

where we were going to live. Everything about it reminded her of Highfield Hall, her old home in Flintshire, except that it was about half the size, which was just about right. I had no connection with County Kildare apart from Punchestown whiskey, a golden spirit once marketed by my great uncle, very much to his profit.

Celbridge Lodge had been a rectory for only seventy years. Before that, it had gone through a period when people 'took it for the hunting' or it was let to officers' families stationed on the Curragh. The man who built the house in the first years of Queen Victoria's reign was Giles Shaw, miller and uncle of Sarah Eliza Shaw, wife of Thomas Conolly, MP for Donegal. Another former occupant, Lionel Fletcher, was said to combine the callings of 'sporting clergyman' with successful horse-dealing. He also had a taste for scratching his initials on the window-glass, and years later I pointed this out to his distinguished great-nephew, Grey Gowrie, chairman of Sotheby's in London.

Plumbing had been installed in 1910 and the manhole covers advertised the fact that 'Cromer, Contractor, Lucan' was responsible. The firm is still in business and Mr William Cromer took us under his wing, having pinpointed several alarming features that needed instant attention. There was a vast water tank in the roof, around which the timbers had rotted. 'It is due to fall down through the house, at any moment now,' announced Mr Cromer cheerfully.

In the 1960s, the influence on interior decoration of Desmond and Mariga Guinness had spread to London via various young interior designers who stayed at Leixlip, and consequently the Chelsea friend who helped us at Celbridge was 'all for colour'. Work was still going on after we moved in, and one elderly painter kept saying 'Good morning, sir' to my father-in-law's portrait, which stood in the corner. When we urged Mr Cromer to speed things up, an additional, very young painter appeared on Monday morning, looking decidedly familiar. 'Did I see you leading a horse in the ring at the Curragh on Saturday?' I enquired. The new recruit nodded and drew me into the conspiracy by putting a finger to his lips. Just then, some bantam hens came racing into the house to pick up crumbs under the dining-room table, and both painters laid down their brushes to give chase.

Every morning an enchanting girl named Regina brought the milk, and we were also blessed with the sort of domestic help that I remembered and feared no longer existed. Our children adored Mrs Timmons who took them 'to gather sticks for the fire' and told them about the 'wee people' and the ghostly hound of Pickering Forest. Pickering was the home of Mabel, Lady Brooke who was a great character, and had the rare distinction of being the only woman in these islands who could claim to be the daughter of a man who was born the year before the Battle of Waterloo. Her drawing room was one of those grand and little-used Irish rooms carelessly built onto the side of a house, with no foundations *whatsoever*. Before a party, the first objective was to dry out the carpet, and a fire was kept burning night and day while steam gently misted over the eighteenth-century chandelier and mirror glass. When the room filled with people, little droplets of condensation fell unnoticed from the ceiling.

Left: *Henry McDowell's work as a genealogist requires an extensive reference library, which is housed in this room. Visitors from all over the world in pursuit of Irish roots are entertained by the McDowells at Celbridge.*

Above: *Oak leaves, the emblem of County Kildare, are depicted in the plasterwork cornice of the dining room. The portrait of Joan McDowell's mother, hanging above the chimneypiece between two elegant candle brackets, is by John Berry. The table is set for luncheon and decorated with an Irish silver potato ring filled with roses.*

Previous page: *A large arrangement of flowers fills a corner of the sitting room. Small pictures by Sir John Lavery and William Sadler, together with a pastel of the children's first pony, Tiny, hang close together on the pale, primrose-yellow walls. The elegant gilt mirror on the adjoining wall is Regency.*

As strangers, we were most kindly received. At Bishopscourt we found my cousin, the junior dean of Trinity, staying with the McGillycuddys, and up at Castletown, Lady Lauderdale was heard to ask her Conolly-Carew grandchildren, 'Are the scones hot?' 'No, Granny.' 'Are they today's?' 'No, Granny.' 'Then I shall have some of the Christmas cake, and *not the mousey side*.'

I began to go to country-house auctions and George, who helped us in the garden, examined my purchases with interest. One day I bought a huge wooden wheelbarrow with extra sides for collecting fallen leaves. 'That,' said George, 'is just like the one I had when I worked at Castlesize, thirty years ago.' It was the same wheelbarrow.

In London, we had a dog named Kimble who was very out-going and made friends with lots of other dogs and their owners in the King's Road. (Through him I got to know Sarah Miles and Katie Boyle.) On Irish soil, Kimble – a Welsh collie – enjoyed life without collar and lead, and in no

Above: The sitting room is a pretty room decorated in the traditional country-house idiom. The eighteenth-century tallboy to the right of the fireplace comes from Henry McDowell's old home. Above it, the portrait of a flower seller is by James Sant, who was appointed painter-in-ordinary to Queen Victoria in 1871.

Right, top: Like many Irish houses of the early Victorian period, Celbridge Lodge was built with the revived enthusiasm for classical proportion; it was variously let to army officers stationed on the Curragh nearby, or 'for the hunting'; then, for seventy years, it was a rectory. No door bell is necessary when all seven dogs charge out to meet every arrival.

Above: *In the hall a plaster bracket in the shape of a heron and supporting a Chinese vase surmounts an old Spanish leather screen from Belgard Castle, seat of the Maude family. The much-used log basket is redolent of the attempt to keep the cold of an old Irish house in winter at bay.*

time at all there were pups in Celbridge who looked exactly like him. Joan's involvement with the County Kildare and West Wicklow branch of the Society for the Prevention of Cruelty to Animals, meant that there was a steady stream of stray dogs lodged in the stables. Finding homes for them was a difficult task, and the longer they stayed the more likely it became that they moved into the house. 'It is more usual, in this country, to have half a dozen *children*,' remarked a disapproving neighbour. Our dog population has now grown to seven. The latest arrival is a large terrier, who looks very nineteenth-century like the dog on the old His Master's Voice label. There exists a photograph of Celbridge Lodge taken about ninety years ago, and outside on the gravel sits just such a terrier. As a genealogist, I cannot help wondering if the newest addition to our motley pack is a descendant of the dog in the picture. Thoughts of this kind give me a comfortable sense of continuity.

Over the years, many American and Australian clients have come to lunch, tea or dinner at Celbridge. Usually research into their Irish ancestry has already been completed and they are making a special trip in order to see all the places connected with the family, and perhaps meet a cousin or two. We always give them traditional food such as salmon or Irish stew, sometimes followed by the wonderful Tipperary cheese called Cashel Blue, and they seem to enjoy coming to an Irish house. Our elder daughter teaches cooking at the Cordon Bleu school in London, and when she comes home she likes nothing better than to go out and pick fresh fruit or vegetables and make something delicious. Last August there were fat blackberries growing on a hillside in County Waterford where we were staying by the sea. These were used instead of the more usual strawberries in the following recipe.

EMILY'S PUDDING

6–8 peaches	*450 g (1 lb) blackberries*
lemon juice	*icing* or *confectioner's sugar, to taste*

FOR THE SAUCE

150 ml (5 fl oz) natural yoghurt	*zest of 1 orange*
150 ml (5 fl oz) cream	*icing* or *confectioner's sugar, to taste*

Serves 4–6

Put the peaches into boiling water for 8 seconds and then plunge them into cold water. Skin them and cut them in half, then return them to a bowl of water with some lemon juice stirred in.

To prepare the purée, simmer the blackberries on their own, without water, and pass them through a nylon sieve. Sweeten and thicken the purée with the sugar. Arrange the peach halves face down in a shallow serving dish and coat with the purée. Chill in the fridge.

To prepare the sauce, mix the yoghurt, cream and orange zest and sweeten to taste with the sugar. Serve it in a sauce boat.

MRS VINCENT O'BRIEN

BALLYDOYLE

County Tipperary

Vincent first saw Ballydoyle one summer evening in 1950. The square Georgian farmhouse stood on a rise at the top of a long, tree-lined avenue, the velvet-green fields of the Golden Vale of County Tipperary sloping away to the foothills of three mountain ranges, the Comeraghs, Knockmealdowns and Galtee Mountains. 'This is the place I will buy,' he said to his brother, Dermot. 'Even the horses will appreciate such beautiful surroundings and the slopes will make perfect gallops!'

Vincent grew up on a farm in Churchtown, County Cork, and trained there for a few years. This locality was already famous for the Cahirmee horse fair, at which Napoleon's favourite horse, Marengo, was bought. From Clashganniff House, Hatton's Grace, Cottage Rake and many other horses went by road, rail and boat to capture some of the biggest National Hunt races in England, including a treble of the three most important races at Cheltenham – only achieved once before. The home farm belonged to Vincent's eldest step-brother and he wanted to find a place of his own. He searched Kildare and Meath, but did not like the flat land where the view was the boundary fence of each field.

Ballydoyle had been the home of the Sadler family – there were seven daughters. Their father, who was an auctioneer, must have loved trees, because each time he made a good deal, he planted a copper beech and the house is surrounded by them. Bacchus was supposed to have drunk from a beech bowl and stained the leaves with his wine.

No horses had been bred or trained at Ballydoyle, and the farm had the chequered fields bounded by ditches typical of County Tipperary. It was set in the heart of the hunting country, which perhaps was another reason

Vincent chose this location. There is a breathtaking view of the Galtee
Mountains and a Derby winner carried the name of the highest peak,
Galteemore. Vincent is trying for the name Galteebeg, the name of the
second highest peak, in case history repeats itself.

When the deal had been completed, Vincent set to work to build the
stables and moved in after Cheltenham in 1951. The construction work
was done by John A. Wood, from Cork, who had a number of horses in
training. One of the best known was Lucky Dome, tiny but full of
courage, who won the Leopardstown Chase. People are always surprised
that the stables are so close to the house but, for Vincent, horses were as
much a part of his life as the books in the library and he wanted to have
them within sight. We have planted the yard with roses and from the
kitchen or dining room, it is lovely to watch the horses' heads over the
stable doors, nodding impatiently before feeding time as the sound of the
barrow is heard. Some wait silently; others snort with irritation at delays.

Tipperary seemed a long way from the sheep station in Australia,
where I grew up and, when Vincent brought me to see Ballydoyle, I was
amazed at the contrast between the rich fertile limestone land and the dry
red earth of home. During the first few years of our marriage, the horses
certainly had a better deal than we did as the stables were finished before
the house was furnished or the garden begun.

Since then, every time we have made a little money or had another
baby, we have built an extra room – always with the largest possible
windows to catch the sun. If we had anticipated how far back the house
would stretch, we would perhaps have planned it differently. It is a very
friendly house and I like the low ceilings and the rooms which are not too
big or grand. Probably my favourite is the dining room, furnished in soft
brown colours to suit the many paintings of Vincent's winners. I can
hardly believe that so many classic winners came from here.

We are fortunate to have our children and twelve grandchildren
nearby and there is always plenty of room for the family celebrations
such as weddings, birthdays and Christmas. The older ones love to watch
the horses with Vincent, and he goes to great lengths to show them the
points that make a champion.

Life in a training stable is geared to hard work but we do not have to
start too early in the morning. The boys arrive at 8.00 am and the horses
pull out at 8.30 to the sound of an old ship's bell. Because we train at
home, there is not the necessity for hurry found at public training
grounds or racecourses where all work has to be finished by a certain
time. It is an enormous advantage to have private gallops and to be able to
please ourselves. We also have all-weather gallops which are essential
when the ground is heavy.

Breakfast is usually before 8.00 am, and Vincent sees two lots of horses
out each morning with a quick cup of tea between. The gallops are laid
out around the house and cover about one and three-quarter miles of
specially treated turf. The objective is to get a consistent surface for horses
regardless of what the weather is doing to the grass. The gallops are
looked after most carefully and several men continually replace
tracks. Two of them are prominent Irish long-distance runners
– replacing divots does wonders for the leg muscles! The terrain

Left: *Paintings of Vincent O'Brien's winners hang in heavy gilt frames on the walls of the dining room which are painted a pale apricot. The curtains and carpet are in soft shades of brown and complement the tones in the paintings. Centrally placed above a side table hangs a painting of Vincent O'Brien with one of his most famous horses, Nijinsky.*

Previous page: *The long, square front of Ballydoyle House, with its glass porch supported by Ionic columns and elegant sash windows surrounded by a thriving virginia creeper, can be seen at the top of the tree-lined avenue leading up to the house. Set on a rise, the house has breathtaking views of the Galtee Mountains.*

is undulating and the horses are worked uphill to get them fit with the minimum of stress on their legs.

We are lucky to have one of the old Norman castles standing in a very rich field; the lumps and humps around it show where the old buildings were. We found a shallow grave with skeletons – probably from a time of famine – and several old iron tools.

Most afternoons are spent looking at the mares and foals, checking gallops and farm and looking around the horses in training. The boys groom the horses, tidy and sweep the stables and yards and, by 4.00 pm, everything is shining and spotless. Each boy looks after two horses and rides out as well. Friday afternoons are important. The horses are weighed and Vincent has a special place beyond the weighing scales where each horse is inspected. Weighing time is interesting for visitors as Vincent comments on each of the horses. He does this after an extremely careful examination, with an intensity that is almost tangible. There seems to be some kind of telepathy between animal and man. A friend of mine watching the weighing said, 'Vincent looks with such concentration, you would be afraid to speak in case you break the spell. It is as if he's psyching out the horses – you almost feel the horse is telling him "I feel this way or that". Even if the horse didn't say, he could draw it out!'

We are lucky with our staff of about sixty. Many of them have been at Ballydoyle for years and most are married with houses on the farm. It is one of the great advantages of living away from other centres that we do not have factories and other stables with which to compete. It would be hard to find a better staff anywhere in the world and I feel this is one of the reasons Vincent has stayed in Ireland.

Entertaining at Ballydoyle is frequently done at breakfast time because our guests are likely to want to see the horses working. I have been fortunate in having a wonderful couple to help me in this – Nora and Alan Rapier. Nora is a magnificent cook and takes care of all our parties and those of our children, while Alan does a great job in the garden and is able to arrange flowers far better than I could. He is a trained designer and people come from afar to see our village church with its splendid Christmas decorations.

When Vincent bought Ballydoyle there were lovely trees but no garden. The fields and laurels came up to the house. Making the garden was a great joy although, coming from Australia, I knew very little about gardening in Ireland. We had one good slope for a rockery and we later planned a wood garden where fritillaries and wood bulbs bloom in spring. Very soon after I came, I was given a brown paper bag of snowdrop bulbs and every year we have divided the plants. They now line the long avenue and are quite a feature during the winter.

In spring we have a sea of daffodils of every conceivable variety. One of our wedding presents was a collection of bulbs from Lionel Richardson, the famous daffodil grower from Waterford. I have always tried to keep buying new varieties each year and never cease to appreciate their wonderful brightness after the gloom of the winter.

Our most treasured possession in the garden is a magnolia, which is now creeping into the drawing room. Its branches have already crossed a terrace and it stands in front of a huge copper beech which provides a

Above: *The Golden Vale of County Tipperary slopes away to give beautiful views across fields full of ripening barley and dotted with sheep. In the distance a medieval ruin on top of a small hill – the Rock of Cashel – looms out of the mist, its silhouette clear against the horizon.*

wonderful backdrop, especially when the early leaves of the copper are almost pale pink. I have been building up patches of rhododendrons and azaleas and find they grow quite well in some parts of the garden, which is surprising in this limestone area. Arthur Shackleton and Richard Bisgrove have helped me in the choice of plants and the general planning.

For some years I have been interested in photography and taking pictures of horses has given me a reason and excuse to spend far more time on this pursuit than I could otherwise have justified. I find the early morning is the ideal time to work in the darkroom, before the telephone starts to ring. What started off as a hobby has now become something of a business, and I provide pictures of the current crop of horses as well as shots of personalities and travels. Over the years many world-famous photographers have come to Ballydoyle and I have picked up quite a few tips by watching and asking questions.

Living in Tipperary had one disadvantage – for both the horses and ourselves – and that was the time it took to get to race meetings. We have overcome this difficulty for the horses by having a runway and a small Skyvan which flies from here to England or France in a couple of hours. Our own lives have been made much easier with a helicopter, as constant driving to race meetings was very time-consuming.

I have long since accepted that at Ballydoyle there is no such thing as a typical day. I dread any sort of organization because plans are bound to be disrupted by a more immediate crisis. Vincent has always maintained that you have to be flexible in your thinking about horses. We might be set for a smart English race meeting one day, and it is all off the next. Horses come first and, if Vincent does not feel a horse should run, no amount of planning or persuasion will make him change his mind.

Above: *The gallops, laid out around the house, cover about one and three-quarter miles of specially treated turf. The horses are trained every morning and work uphill on the gentle gradients which gets them fit with the minimum amount of stress on their legs. They are seen here at a corner which closely resembles the Tattenham corner at the Derby.*

Most of our entertaining is done for people who are connected with horse racing or breeding – whether owners, their friends or other visitors. We have a number of overseas visitors from the United States, Britain, France, Australia and the Middle East, and it has always been the greatest pleasure to be able to meet many of the outstanding people who have been drawn towards horses and racing after they have made a success of their own businesses. Among those I would put Charlie Engelhard, owner of Nijinsky, a fascinating, amusing man, and his talented wife, Jane; also John McShain, one of the great builders of America who was responsible for restoring the White House, building the Pentagon, the Lincoln Memorial and the cathedral in Washington (John's father came from the north of Ireland and started as a carpenter in America); John Galbreath, another of America's builders and owner of Roberto; Raymond Guest, ambassador to Ireland with his wife Caroline, who was a descendant of one of Napoleon's generals; and Jack Mulcahy, a real Irishman and a man who always brings joy to the day.

More recently we have trained horses for Robert Sangster whose knowledge of his immense string, their breeding and whereabouts continually astonishes me; for Stavros Niarchos and his daughter Maria who run their empire most efficiently and from whose business acumen we have been able to learn so much; and for Sheikh Mohammed al Maktoum, who has visited Ballydoyle. Thanks to him, I was able to spend a few days photographing in the great desert of the Empty Quarter, between the United Arab Emirates and Saudia Arabia.

As I finish, the bell for the evening feed rings. The lights will soon go down in the yard and the horses will settle for the night. Vincent has come into his study and is preparing the worksheet for the morning. Is his seventh Derby winner there? Only time will tell.

Top: The conservatory with large, sliding glass doors looks out onto the tall shrubs and trees in the garden. Informal cane furniture covered in a boldly patterned fabric, a pale rug and the bar in one corner make this a bright, cheerful room where the O'Briens entertain in the summer and on warm days in the winter.

Above: As the stables are built close to the house, the O'Briens can see the horses' heads over the stable doors from the kitchen and dining room. Jacqueline O'Brien's photography started as a hobby but has now become something of a business; she provides current pictures of horses and personalities involved with horses.

Opposite: Pale yellow is the dominant colour of the sitting room, where sunlight streams in through the large windows with their southern aspect and views across the mountains. As with most of the rooms at Ballydoyle, the sitting room is of a comfortable size and, with its long, low ceiling, retains much of the charm of the original Georgian farmhouse.

We have always liked the best Irish food and tend to concentrate on lamb, beef, salmon and shellfish, with vegetables and fruit from our kitchen garden. With new business associates we try and find out what they like to eat and drink in advance.

Here is a recipe for biscuits which we often serve with coffee – a recipe I brought with me from Australia.

CORNFLAKE BISCUITS

100 g (4 oz/½ cup) castor or superfine sugar
75 g (3 oz/6 tablespoons) margarine
1 egg, beaten

100 g (4 oz/¾ cup) self-raising flour
pinch salt
cornflakes

Preheat the oven to 180°C (350°F, gas mark 4).

Cream the sugar and margarine. Add the well-beaten egg. Sift the flour and salt and fold in lightly but well. Roll a teaspoonful of the mixture in cornflakes, place on a greased baking tray and leave to bake for 15 minutes. They should be flat and crisp.

MRS PYERS O'CONOR-NASH

CLONALIS
*County
Roscommon*

If you were reading any tourist guide to Ireland, you would find Clonalis described more or less as follows:

Clonalis is the ancestral home of the O'Conors of Connaught, descendants of the last high kings of Ireland and traditional kings of Connaught. It is situated in the heart of the O'Conor land, that is territory associated with the O'Conors for hundreds of years before the Anglo-Norman invasion in 1169. The O'Conor family is the oldest family in Europe. A total of ninety-six generations which trace their earliest ancestors back to Milesian times, around 1100 BC. This is borne out by the beautifully executed family pedigree in the library signed by Sir William Betham, Ulster King of Arms, 1825. There is a detailed table of descent of the O'Conor family, in direct, male legitimate line from the year *c*.75.

To us, Clonalis has become home.

My husband Pyers and I, together with our two children, arrived in Clonalis just six years ago, following the death of my husband's uncle, Reverend Charles O'Conor, SJ, O'Conor Don, and at the request of my mother-in-law, Gertrude. It was early December and the temperature was well below freezing point. During our first night, there was a heavy snowfall. When we awoke the following morning, the fields and trees in the grounds outside looked so pretty, but inside it was bitterly cold and our water was frozen. I began to have doubts about the task we had undertaken.

Above: *The coronation stone of the O'Conors of Connaught was brought from Rathcroghan in County Roscommon. One of the last to be crowned king of Connaught was Felim O'Conor, killed in the battle of Athenry against his Connaught neighbours the de Burghs and the de Berminghams in 1316.*

Previous page: *Some of the oldest documents from the O'Conor archives, including the last judgement handed down by the Brehon lawmakers, are displayed in the library. Other documents including letters and family papers signed by, amongst others, Charles II, Louis XIV, William Gladstone and Daniel O'Connell, are displayed in the billiard room.*

Many problems confronted us during our first years in the house. Our main concern was the survival of Clonalis: how to ensure its future and how to meet the crippling demands of inheritance taxes without having to sever Clonalis from its treasures – the archives, the library, the paintings and the harp that belonged to the eighteenth-century bard, Carolan. (It is said that he played sweeter music for the O'Conors than for any other family.) These things are the very heart of Clonalis; without them the house would die. During the following two years my husband spent much time in negotiation with various government ministers and sold a considerable amount of land to meet the demands of the revenue commissioners. Then, to our great relief and delight, the 1984 Finance Act was amended, and this helped to lessen the tax bill.

The present Clonalis house is not very old; it was designed in Victorian Italianate style by Pepys Cockrell and built in 1875. It succeeded many other O'Conor houses and castles. Turlough Mor O'Connor, the high king of Ireland who reigned from 1119 to 1156, built the first stone castles in Ireland. He also commissioned the Cross of Cong, which contains a relic of the True Cross and is one of the most magnificent works of Irish art. It is now housed in the National Museum in Dublin.

When we arrived we had two small children and we very much wanted to create a home for them. The house was structurally sound but in dire need of reorganization and redecoration. The kitchen and pantries were located some distance away from the main rooms, as was the custom in the nineteenth century when there was no shortage of domestic staff to clean and cook and wait at table. They were smaller than the rooms in the main part of the house, and consequently easier to keep warm in winter, so we decided to turn them into living quarters for the family. The main kitchen became a sitting room, while two pantries were made into a modern kitchen. The old servants' dining room became a play room and, having rewired this section we installed a washing machine – the first such labour-saving device to be introduced in Clonalis since it was built. We felt that at last the house had moved into the twentieth century! This family area is heated very effectively by a solid-fuel heating system, using peat from our own bogs.

When we finished decorating our living quarters, we began to assess the amount of work we would have to do in the main rooms. We were lucky to meet a young man from Castlerea who over the next three years painted and papered nearly every room in the house. The entrance hall with its Ionic columns of pink Mallow marble, was the first. The O'Conor Dons, as the descendants of kings of the old order, continued as hereditary standard bearers of Ireland. The blue standard of St Patrick bearing the golden harp hangs in this entrance hall and was last carried in 1911, at the coronation of King George V.

The main reception rooms, which include the drawing room, the library and the dining room, all face south-west, and when the sun shines they are full of light. The drawing room has a chimney piece at either end of the room; they are made from Siena marble and were removed from the eighteenth-century mansion which preceded this present house. The furniture is mainly Victorian and there are some nice pieces of Meissen china as decorative objects. The dining room is rather a formal room, furnished with Irish Sheraton furniture which was designed and made for the house when it was built. The walls are hung with the portraits of eleven male members of the O'Conor family, representing seven different continuous generations.

At first, the portraits appeared quite formidable to me but, as I became familiar with each of them and became aware of their achievements, I began to feel that I knew them all personally! The earliest portrait is that of Denis O'Conor (1674–1750). In 1720 he was rendered destitute by forfeiture in the wake of the Williamite wars. He went forward to fight a historic law case which resulted in a portion of the O'Conor lands being returned to the family, and being saved from total confiscation during the implementation of the penal laws. Denis's eldest son was Charles O'Conor of Ballinagare. He was an antiquarian, and author of *Dissertations on the History of Ireland* (1764). He was responsible for collecting most of the papers which make up the O'Conor archives. Charles's eldest grandson was Owen O'Conor Don (1763–1831) who became the first Catholic member of parliament for Roscommon, after the granting of Catholic Emancipation. He was succeeded as member for Roscommon by his son and grandson. The latter was Charles Owen O'Conor Don who was a founder member of the Gaelic League. He was responsible for having the Irish language included in the school curriculum, and he built several schools in the area. The O'Conor Don title, meaning 'princely' or 'kingly', was first used in 1385 and is still the title given to the chief of the O'Conor clan.

The name Charles is prevalent in the O'Conor family. Yet another Charles O'Conor, of Mount Allen, emigrated to the United States following the failure of the 1798 rebellion. His grandson became known as Charles O'Conor of New York and in 1872 was the first Catholic nominated to the United States presidency. He ran against Ulysses Grant; of course, Grant won that election.

One of the reasons we are so proud of our O'Conor history is that we are one of the few families in Europe that can trace descent from the first century AD.

Below: *The crest and motto of the O'Conor family are fixed to the entrance gates at Clonalis. The motto reads in Irish, O DHIA GACH CÚCABRACH – From God Comes Our Strength. The crest of a mailed forearm brandishing a sword attests to earlier warlike feats.*

Feredach the Just RH★	c. 75
Fiacha Finnola RH	c. 95
Tuathal Techmar RH	c. 130
Felim the Lawgiver	c. 164
Conn of the 100 Battles RH	c. 177
Art the Solitary RH	c. 195
Cormac RH	c. 227
Cairbre Liffechair RH	284
Fiacha Sraiftene RH	322
Murchertagh Fireach RH	356
Eochy Moymedon RH	366
Brian RC†	397
Duagh Galach RC	438
Eoghan Shreve (never king)	464
Muiredhach Mal (never king)	489

Above: *A penal law chalice dating from 1722 stands on a richly embroidered silk vestment. Both were used by Bishop Thaddeus O'Rourke in contravention of the anti-Catholic laws following the Williamite wars. The chalice was consecrated at an open-air mass in Kilmactranny, County Sligo.*

Opposite: *The entrance hall of Clonalis is dominated by columns of pink Mallow marble. In this hall hangs the blue standard of St Patrick bearing the golden harp, last carried at the coronation of King George V. The young boy standing in the centre portrait was to become Charles Owen O'Conor Don MP, who built the present Clonalis in the late 1870s in place of an earlier Georgian house.*

Fergus RC	517
Eochy Termacherna RC.	543
Hugh (Aedh) RC	577
Uada RC .	599
Roghallach RC	645
Fergus RC	649
Muiredhach Muilethan RC .	700
Innrechtach (Enright) RC	751
Murgil (never king) .	774
Tomaltach (never king) .	810
Muirgis RC .	723
Teige (never king)	841
Concovar (Conor) RC .	879
Cathal RC	925
Teige of the Three Towers RC	954
Conor RC	971
Cathal RC .	1010
Teige of the White Steed RC	1030
Hugh of the Broken Spear RC	1067
Roderic (Rory of the Yellow Hound) RC	1105
Turlough Mor O'Connor RH	1156
Cathal Crovedearg RC .	1224
Hugh RC.	1228
Roderick (Rory) (never king)	1244
Owen RC	1274
Hugh RC.	1309
Turlough RC	1345
Hugh RC.	1356
Turlough Oge (first O'Connor Don)	1406
Felim Geancach	1474
Owen Gaech .	1485
Carbry	1546
Dermot	1585
Sir Hugh .	1632
Cahill Oge	1634
Charles	1696
Denis .	1750
Charles	1790
Denis .	1804
Owen MP	1831
Denis MP.	1847
Charles Owen MP	1905
Denis Charles	1917
Owen .	1943
Charles Reverend SJ .	1981
Denis .	now living

★RH Rex Hiberniae (king of Ireland)
†RC Rex Connachtia (king of Connacht)

We are very privileged to have a chapel in the house. The altar was taken from the original eighteenth-century mansion, and is known as a penal altar as it dates from a period in Irish history when Mass had to be celebrated in secret. On the altar is a pectoral cross and ring which belonged to Bishop Thaddeus O'Rourke; it had been presented to him by Prince Eugene of Savoy. Bishop O'Rourke's chalice is also here; he consecrated it in 1722. The family had two important privileges at that time: they had the right to preserve the Blessed Sacrament in the house and to appoint the parish priest of Castlerea and Ballintubber (County Roscommon), but these privileges were abolished following Vatican II. Mass is still celebrated several times a year in the chapel and last April our daughter Letitia was christened here. Letitia was born in March 1987; she is the first baby in Clonalis for over 110 years.

We no longer use the billiard room for its designated purpose. It now contains glass cases housing documents and papers which can be viewed by the public when the house is open during the summer months. The oldest manuscript is the last verdict handed down by the Brehon lawmakers; it dates from the sixteenth century. The Brehon laws were the ancient gaelic laws of Ireland.

The archives also contain at least 100,000 letters and documents representing personal, social, business and political correspondence. There are legal documents, diaries, journals, account books, and drafts of speeches and essays, together with minutes of meetings of eighteenth- and nineteenth-century organizations of historical importance. These are memoranda of generations of men and women of various social backgrounds, chiefly from Ireland, but also from England, France, Italy, South America, Canada, Australia and the United States. Many of the letters are from Douglas Hyde, who was the first president of Ireland, a neighbour of the O'Conors and a close personal friend.

My favourite of all the rooms in the house is the library. It is a peaceful, cosy room which, even if the weather is dull and grey, is still full of warmth and charm. The oldest book in the library dates from the middle of the seventeenth century. By just glancing at the shelves you can very quickly learn the interests different members of the family pursued, down through the centuries. I must admit that my 1980s paperbacks are not to be found in this tranquil room.

An interesting portrait hangs over the chimney piece in the library. It is of the Reverend Charles O'Conor (1764–1828), who translated into Latin the Annals of the Four Masters. He was chaplain to the Marquis of Buckinghamshire's wife. Just below is a photograph of Father Charles O'Conor, SJ, O'Conor Don; he lived from 1905 to 1981. He is pictured with the famous Cross of Cong commissioned by Turlough Mor O'Connor. As Father O'Conor was a direct descendant of Turlough Mor, this photograph spans twenty-four generations.

In order to generate income for the upkeep of Clonalis, the house is open to the public during the summer months. Also, it gives us an opportunity to share the history of this unique Gaelic family with others. People often ask us if we find the public an intrusion in our lives and the answer is, simply, no. We believe that, as it goes back so far and includes the names of men well known in this country, the history of the O'Conor

Left: *A four-poster bed with ornate hangings stands in a guest bedroom. The fine bedspread was embroidered by nuns in Mountmellick about ninety years ago. A Sèvres clock stands on the mid nineteenth-century mantelpiece of Siena marble.*

Above: *The dining-room table is set with a Mason ironstone service. The palm tree epergnes in plated silver are variously decorated with camels and Irish wolfhounds and were exhibited at the great nineteenth-century Crystal Palace exhibition in London.*

Above: *The late Reverend Father Charles O'Conor, SJ, O'Conor Don, was photographed in the National Museum in Dublin beside the Cross of Cong commissioned c. 1156 by his direct ancestor Turlough Mor O'Connor when he was high king of Ireland. The photograph thus spans twenty-four generations of O'Conors.*

family is very much the history of Ireland; the letters and documents recording the trials, tribulations, and joys also, of Irish people.

Now, as we approach the end of the 1980s, Clonalis is very much a family home. The voices of our young children and their friends echo through the rooms. We are aware that the children are developing a sense of history and pride in their heritage and we hope that this will continue to grow and that they will come to love Clonalis and its contents, and in their turn help it to survive well into the twenty-first century.

Whereas unusual and exotic foodstuffs are not always available in our local shops, as a compensation salmon during the season is brought to me by the ghillie, just hours after it is caught. I usually poach the whole salmon, and serve it simply with home-made mayonnaise, new potatoes and fresh vegetables from our garden.

Also from about mid March until July, we have beautiful tender lamb from our own flock. This too I cook simply, because the meat itself is of such high quality.

ROAST LAMB

leg of lamb
salt
black pepper

few sprigs rosemary
few cloves garlic or *sprigs parsley*

After covering the leg of lamb with salt and grated black pepper, I find placing a few sprigs of rosemary beneath and around the joint in the pan greatly adds to the flavour. I also insert small pieces of garlic into the fatty portion of the joint and near the bone; this not only helps to make the meat more tender, but the flavour gently permeating the meat is not strong and is generally liked. Another old-fashioned trick is to make as many as 20 incisions into the meat with a sharply pointed knife, and to insert stalks or small sprigs of parsley. These must be well pressed in with a knife, for if any remain on the surface they will become burnt during the roasting.

Roast the leg at 190°C (375°F, gas mark 5) for 15 minutes per 450 g (1 lb) and an extra 15 minutes.

On a cold wet day, of which there are many in County Roscommon, I often encourage the children to make toffee and fudge in the warmth and comfort of the kitchen. Here are some of the recipes we use.

CHOCOLATE FUDGE

900 g (2 lb) sugar, brown or *white*
275 ml (10 fl oz) milk
100 g (4 oz/½ cup) butter
65 g (3 heaping tablespoons) grated chocolate

grated rind and juice of an orange
a few drops vanilla essence or *extract*

Put the sugar and milk to soak for one hour. Bring to the boil slowly with all the other ingredients, except the vanilla. Once boiling, boil fast for 10 to 15 minutes. The mixture will rise in the saucepan; do not stir more than is absolutely necessary to keep it from burning. Take the pan off the heat when the mixture begins to sink and crystallize on the edge of the pan. Do not stir for 2 minutes, then add the vanilla and beat the mixture with a wooden spoon to the consistency of thick cream. Pour it quickly into a well-buttered tin or pan, and allow to cool. Score the top with a knife when it is half cold.

HOME-MADE TOFFEE

350 g (12 oz/2 cups) demerara or *raw sugar*
200 g (7 fl oz/½ cup) golden or *dark corn syrup*
225 g (8 oz/1 cup) butter
grated rind and juice of half a lemon

Boil all the ingredients together and test for setting: a small quantity dropped into cold water should harden at once. Pour onto an oiled tin or pan. When barely set, score the top with a knife and loosen from the tin. Leave until firm before breaking into pieces. Store in an air-tight tin or container.

For Christmas and other feasts of celebration, we make these more elaborate offerings.

TRUFFLES

225 g (8 oz) dark or *semi-sweet chocolate*
10 ml (2 teaspoons) rum
4 egg yolks, beaten
50 g (2 oz/⅓ cup) vermicelli or *chocolate sprinkles*
40 g (1½ oz/3 tablespoons) butter
10 g (2 teaspoons) icing or *confectioner's sugar*
10 ml (2 teaspoons) double or *heavy cream, lightly whipped*
10 g (2 teaspoons) cocoa powder

Break the chocolate into small pieces, place them in a bowl over a saucepan of hot water and allow to melt. Stir in the beaten egg yolks, butter, lightly whipped double *or* heavy cream and rum. Remove the bowl from the saucepan and allow to cool. Roll teaspoonfuls of the mixture each into small balls. Coat half with the vermicelli *or* chocolate sprinkles, and dip the rest in a mixture of the icing *or* confectioner's sugar and cocoa powder.

RUM CHERRIES

100 g (4 oz/½ cup) glacé cherries
225 g (8 oz) dark or *semi-sweet chocolate*
65 ml (2½ fl oz) rum

Place the glacé cherries in a screw-top jar with the rum and leave for two days. Remove and drain well. Melt the chocolate in a bowl over hot water. Spear the cherries onto skewers and dip them in the chocolate, coating them completely. Place them on greaseproof paper until set. Remove skewers.

Above: *The O'Conor family is one of the few in Europe that can trace its descent from the first century AD. The O'Conor Don title, meaning 'princely' or 'kingly', was first used in 1385 and is still the title given to the chief of the O'Conor clan.*

BIRR CASTLE
County Offaly

When we came back to Birr it was summer. In the long evenings, as the shadows of the trees slant across the lawn and the sun shines in through the front door, Birr looks at its most enchanted. We had been living in Algeria and returned on the death of my father-in-law, most of our married life having been spent wandering round the world on the various UN assignments that had taken my husband from West Africa to Bangladesh and other places in between. This, I suppose, had made us and our two older children adaptable. They, like us, had lived in tents with the Bakhtiari in Iran, been on desert expeditions in the Sahara and enjoyed picnics on the edge of the jungles and on the beaches of Bangladesh. I had already moved house five times. We were, therefore, happy to settle down and feel at home, at last.

On those summer evenings I wandered around the house remembering how, in my parents-in-law's time, it had been full of life. It now seemed so big and so silent – except for the distant rush of the river and those other more mysterious crackings in the woodwork making me jump: sighs and creaks like a ship at sea. It occurred to me that the house had a presence, expectant but not unfriendly.

Now, I have come to love the space of it, the long passages and quiet high-ceilinged rooms. In summer the house is at its best and seems to open out, embracing peacefully any number of people of different generations. Winter comes though, and life shrinks to the warmest area, near the fire in the library. The castle looks grey, bleak and forbidding and it is on such a winter afternoon, walking back from the kitchen garden, that I am most likely to be asked by someone visiting the gardens, 'But you can't live in *all* of it?'

Above: *Built over the medieval O'Carroll gate-tower, Birr Castle was gothicized in the last century to conform to the prevailing taste. The original entrance to the O'Carroll fortress was at the top of Castle Street in Birr; over time the gates have been moved further away from the centre of the town.*

Previous page: *A screen, seen through an intricately designed four-poster bed in Anne, Countess of Rosse's bedroom, was painted by Carl Toms to depict members of the family in an idealized landscape based on the Birr demesne. The remains of the observatory erected by the 'telescope earl' can be clearly seen.*

Right, top: *For Lady Rosse, flowers play an important part in the house, and she brings in as many as possible from the castle grounds; this is one of her arrangements in the library. In her mother-in-law's day a tractor would arrive every Friday morning pulling a trailer filled with an avalanche of flowers, and all would be in place by lunchtime. A collection of Turcaman jewellery, collected by Lord and Lady Rosse during their six years in Iran, is arranged on the Irish Georgian dumb waiter.*

Above: *The Countess of Rosse sits at her desk in the small library amidst cookery books, recipes and medicinal hints from the archives which date back to the seventeenth century. An extensive collection of gardening books acquired by the late Earl of Rosse is kept in this room.*

The large amount of space has many advantages, one of which is that nothing needs to be thrown away. I sometimes think nothing *is* thrown away. Unwanted possessions just move further and further from the centre of activity, resurfacing again after many years, as my mother-in-law found to her delight when our clerk of the works admitted he had not, as he had been instructed thirty years before, thrown out the remains of the astronomical equipment, but only put them away further on. They have now been restored and catalogued by the Whipple Museum in Cambridge. Thus, reorganizing a long-unused room can sometimes assume almost archaeological significance. Remove the upper layer – perhaps the debris of flower arranging and old Christmas decorations – to find beneath them layer two – wooden boats and broken croquet mallets from a childhood long past. Below that, mysterious fencing masks and brass bells – is this perhaps Uncle Geoffrey, or are we earlier still? Also, we have uncovered the complete photographic darkroom of Mary Rosse, the third Countess, who worked in it in the 1850s.

Now that I know the house better I find I can tell which changes and alterations were made by the different wives. Sometimes I feel I have about a dozen mothers-in-law going back to the seventeenth century. Many of them, or their housekeepers, left cooking recipes and medicinal hints – 300 years worth of cures for children's coughs and 'quaking puddings', ways to polish mahogany tables and make black ink 'such as will never fade'. Our archives, now wonderfully organized thanks to the help of Anthony Malcomson and the North of Ireland Public Records Office, are an endless help to us and to others doing historical research, especially now that we have our annual exhibitions.

It was because we realized so many different facets of life were recorded here – from gardening to astronomy, history to photography, plant hunting and recipes – that the idea seemed irresistible. We started with Uncle Charlie, otherwise known as Sir Charles Parsons, who was the younger brother of the telescope earl and who invented the marine turbine. We were lucky in that the year of our return to Birr coincided with his centenary. Another exhibition was historical, connected with the castle and the town, of which it is always so much a part. We have also had 'The Making of the Gardens', which explained how the gardens came to be as they are now, from the laying out of the park in the seventeenth century and the creation of the lake in the eighteenth, to the present day with my mother-in-law's designs for the Formal Gardens and the planting of rare species by my father-in-law, and the botanical expeditions which were subscribed to. The most successful exhibition so far, in that it has taken off under its own steam and is still touring, having already visited England, Germany and Austria, is the photographic exhibition. It was put on with the help of the Dublin Institute of Technology and describes the work and life of Mary Rosse, my husband's great-great-grandmother, who was one of that select group of pioneer lady photographers.

These exhibitions enable us to show the contents of the house, the chests and cupboards, the basements and store rooms, in an organized way, so that other people can enjoy our 'finds'. From my point of view, the most exhausting part of each exhibition is putting

Top: *The intricately carved oak sideboard in the dining room displays the family crest and coat of arms with heraldic leopards used as supporters. It was designed by Mary, Countess of Rosse, when she extended the room in the 1840s. Judging from its size and weight, it was very probably made in the room in which it stands.*

Above: *This view of the seventeenth-century yew staircase was taken through four floors to the plaster vaulting. Birr Castle is mentioned in Dineley's* Observations on a Voyage through the Kingdom of Ireland, *published in 1681, as having 'the fairest' staircase in the land.*

Opposite: *The yellow drawing-room fireplace has an unusual curtain grate made in the Dublin quays in the eighteenth century. This is one of the few rooms in the castle to retain its eighteenth-century features and plasterwork almost complete. It was restored, the fabric on the walls rehung and much of the furniture brought to the room by Anne, Countess of Rosse.*

everything back again once the excitement is over.

Over the last few years our life seems to have settled into something of a pattern, with the annual exhibition coming in the spring, the international carriage driving in September, and the shoot, and gundog trials in the winter. Also, we now hold in June a concert for the Music Festival in Great Irish Houses. Much of my time seems to be spent – as it was when my husband worked for the United Nations Development Programme – in keeping open house for 'experts': experts on early photography, on botany, on Irish history, tourism, astronomy, on farming and forestry, and even carriage driving. As well as this, we now entertain visitors, often from the United States and elsewhere abroad, who like to see everything, at once if possible, and who we do our best to give lunch to and show round. (My husband is better at this than I am and can be guaranteed to walk almost anyone off their feet.)

We rely very much on our own produce, as has always been the case. As well as vegetables from the kitchen garden, we eat our own venison and, in winter, duck and pheasant. Sometimes I try out some of the old recipes. The ingredients, apart from the more exotic ones such as mace and rose-water, are often much the same as today's. The earliest and perhaps the most interesting cookbook is that of Dorothy Parsons who came to live here on her marriage in 1636. Almost certainly, we are still cooking in her kitchen, a timeless room approached through a doorway that is more like a passage through the ten-foot-wide walls of the gate-tower, and which opens out under seventeenth-century vaulting. Unlike the dining room which, as in many old houses, seems to have changed place over the centuries, the kitchen has stayed in the same room except for one brief expansion into an enormous Victorian basement, now used for the central heating boiler. Our housekeeper, Annie Shortt, who sadly died earlier this year after working here for fifty-six years, remembered well working there. Her memories of recipes and the meals and grand occasions at which they were eaten, stretched back over three generations. One year we will certainly have to have a kitchen and housekeeping exhibition.

As well as the exhibition and other annual events, there is, of course, the garden. A constant source of both delight and worry, there is never a moment when we should not be doing something in it, from rescuing trees covered in ivy to planting out the new shrubs and trees that have been propagated from the expeditions we subscribe to. Unlike the house, the garden is a transitory thing that can change of its own accord if it is not watched and loved and maintained, and there are many arguments over what should be planted up, or allowed to go wild, what chopped down, or which path redirected. The garden comes into the house as much as possible, not only in these theoretical discussions but in the form of garden produce and flowers.

A big house like this seems to need flowers; my mother-in-law was an expert. I remember the tractor appearing early on a Friday morning pulling a trailer filled with an avalanche of flowers. Two gardeners would lay them reverently onto the dust sheets laid out over the Turkish carpets in the hall, the vases already filled with water waiting expectantly. By lunchtime the transformation would be complete and the house

Left: *In Anne, Countess of Rosse's bedroom, the matching suite of highly individual gothic furniture was designed by Mary, Countess of Rosse, in the early nineteenth century, and made and painted by the estate workshops. The cupboards, chests of drawers, four-poster bed and pelmet all display the pinnacle and ropework design.*

Right: *The gothic saloon was built onto the house c. 1810 by the second Earl of Rosse. The Chippendale furniture is reputed to be the last complete documented set of Chippendale furniture still in private hands. It was brought to Birr by Anne, Countess of Rosse, on her marriage in 1935.*

Below: *A rose made by the celebrated stage and costume designer, Oliver Messel (the brother of Anne, Countess of Rosse), for a production of Richard Strauss's opera* Der Rosenkavalier *rests in front of nostalgic childhood photographs including one of Lord Rosse with his younger brother, Martin, and Alison his future wife.*

blossomed with towering flower arrangements, filling the urns, the Sicilian vases and the jardinières in the saloon, flowing over onto tables and desks.

Another yearly event is Vintage Week in Birr which, although based in the town, seems usually to overflow into the castle. The shops in the town bring out their oldest stock from their back store rooms to make the windows as 'vintage' as possible and the town is full of festivities from concerts to singing in the pubs. The castle has always been part of the town, though it is hard to believe it when entering through Mary Rosse's imposing gates and sweeping around the curve of the carriage-drive with its view of the lake and glimpses of the castle through the beech trees. Over the years, as times improved and the town expanded, the gates were moved steadily further and further from the top of Castle Street, the original entrance to the O'Carroll fortress, and now the visitor enters well away from the centre of the town, only to be swept back again, unknowingly, behind the walls where Castle Street is now only visible from the upper floors.

I rely much on the town and its surrounds, as did those seventeenth-century ladies whose cookbooks are so fascinating. I identify with those wives busily keeping herb gardens and still rooms, a sharp eye turned towards the farm, the woods, and the bogs. At least I like to think so. In the early days, as now, jobs were done less for appearances' sake than to

keep life going and to continue to exist here. Their Victorian and Edwardian counterparts, with huge staffs and bombazeen-aproned housekeepers, their shooting parties and amateur dramatics, would, I think, have been all too much for me.

Looking out of the nursery window I can see down into the town and then across to the Slieve Bloom hills, a view that can distract me easily from what I am supposed to be doing. Then I suddenly remember that term has started and it is time to fetch our youngest child from school. I had intended to write about ourselves and our lives here, but I see the house has taken over again. The past, in a house like this, weighs heavily. As Elizabeth Bowen said, 'Every death thickens the atmosphere', and indeed every generation of the family leaves another layer, another collection of books, a new stair carpet, tiles in the pantry or a fireplace in the drawing room. This house was never built in one piece, it grew. In good times it expanded and was beautified inside and out; in the bad times it stayed very much the same apart from, for example, the marks of cannonballs in the stonework.

We feel we cannot keep a house such as this to ourselves. Part of its point is that it must be shared, and with as many people as possible who

Above: *The table set for a meal in the window of the dining room overlooks the private garden. Unusual varieties of fruit and vegetables from the garden, cooked to the instructions of old Birr recipe books are often served, as are venison, duck and pheasant from the castle grounds.*

126

are interested in what it holds, although I admit my feelings on this fluctuate depending on the weather, the state of the deepfreeze and the loudness of the children's stereo. Which brings me to the point that the house was made for living in as a family, for children and their friends – dare I even say, dogs. Surely, somewhere there must always be a sofa that can be bounced on. But I myself love it especially when it is *very* empty and *very* quiet on those long summer evenings.

Here are some recipes and notes selected from the many that have been left in the house by succeeding housekeepers. The first, dated 1666, is from Dorothy Parsons' *Book of Choyce Receipts*.

TO MAKE GOOSEBERY CREAME

Take a pint of gooseberys before they are ripe, put them in a skillet with as much fair water as will cover them and boyle them till they are tender then straine them and putt them into the skillet againe with a quart of swett cream and when they boyle putt to them 5 yolks of eggs well beaten.

Continually stirr them till they are as thick as you would have it then season it and keep it in your dish. If you think it too yellow leave out some of the eggs. Serve it up cold.

Above: *Voltaire and a companion stand guard over a bowl of seeds from some of the rare trees in the demesne collected by Lord Rosse in the autumn. New trees and shrubs are constantly propagated and planted out on the return of plant-hunting expeditions abroad subscribed to by Lord and Lady Rosse.*

This one, which dates from about 1805, is from the recipe book of Alice, Countess of Rosse.

OYSTER SOUP

Slice six onions. Boil them in five pints of water till soft, dry them in a cloth and fry them brown, put them back into the same water with half a pound or less of fresh butter and fifty oysters with their liquour, thicken with the inside of a two penny stale loaf, salt and pepper to your taste, one or two anchovies or a small piece of salt herring well pounded will be an improvement. Fry 8 or 10 oysters and throw them into the soup when ready to dish. N.B. This soup will take 3 hours to simmer slowly after the first boil and should be frequently stirred with a spoon from the bottom.

Finally, this is taken from the notes kept by Cassandra, Countess of Rosse's housekeeper, and dated about 1870.

FOR SEASICKNESS

Take as much cayenne pepper as you can possibly bear in a basin of hot soup and all sickness and nausea will disappear.

127

MR PATRICK SCOTT

BALLYNABROCKY
County Wicklow

I have always been fascinated by cul de sac roads, and I must have driven down hundreds. I particularly like those that exist all around the Irish coast, when the road doesn't just stop but disappears into the sea, like Christo's running fence.

Ballynabrocky (a gaelic word which when translated into English means Townland of the Badgers) is at the end of a road in the Wicklow hills that disappears into a mountain bog.

I bought the house in 1963 just after the snow had melted. It had been a very severe winter, and the road had been closed for ten weeks. The thaw exposed the carcasses of many sheep that had perished, and every green leaf or shoot within 'sheep reach' had been stripped. The house had been lying empty and deserted for about two years, and the animals had used it for shelter.

It is a perfectly straightforward two up, two down farmhouse, but it is built of granite, and the stone has been roughly dressed at the eaves, barges and around the openings, suggesting that one of the masons from the nearby quarry at Ballyknockan was involved in the construction, which, to judge by the window mouldings, would have been during the 1820s.

The farm buildings were equally well built, and I liked the way that they were connected to the house, which made it easy to extend the living area into the stable and long barn.

I made very few structural alterations. I demolished a half-finished lean-to kitchenette and knocked two holes in existing walls to connect the old kitchen with the stable and long barn. I then knocked a door out of the long barn on the south side, but I resisted the temptation to put in

Left: *Looking out from the old kitchen across a valley teeming with badgers, which gave the area its name, this views is of Mount Sorrel where wild sorrel grows prolifically. Originally, five mountain sheep farms stood in the immediate area, sharing grazing rights over 4,000 acres. Only one remains still farming.*

windows facing south because I use the barn for working – away from the temptations of the world outside. Also I have a long-term plan to build a large conservatory on that side.

I did not use a professional builder to carry out any of the alterations, because I felt that I wanted to do as much as possible myself; I enjoy any kind of work that entails making things. I soon enlisted the help of my nearest neighbour, Martin Kearns, who is a farmer but turned out to be an inspired craftsman, and we worked together to make the house habitable again. Truthfully, he did most of the work, quite often helped by his most resourceful wife, Sheila.

I enjoyed the time I spent working with him; it was fun, and he always came up with an ingenious solution to every problem.

I do not live permanently in the house because I have a studio in Dublin, and I find it easier to work there. I suppose this is because there is more 'pressure' to produce in an urban atmosphere. When I am in the country I want to be outside all the time. I was brought up in the country, and my childhood memories are all concerned with being out of doors.

It would be untrue to say that I never work in the country; I sometimes move my studio there to work on a special commission. Also, I have done all my gestural drawings there – I take my clothes off and work out of

Above: *Because of the prevailing wind the only opening in the north wall of the house is this doorway. The new door opens separately from the bottom forming a half-door with a cat flap. This door, from the old kitchen, would have led directly into the farmyard.*

Right: *The new kitchen connects the old kitchen to the long barn, running at right angles to the main house. On the dressers are a collection of decal-edged and spongeware meat dishes. The hen coop seen through the doorway in the long barn was made by a basketmaker in Connemara.*

Previous page: *The old kitchen is now used as a sitting room. A settle bed from the 1820s and mid nineteenth-century famine chairs are in keeping with the rustic architecture of the house and enhanced by the unglazed clay floor tiles made in Athy. Over the fireplace is a clevvy or spit rack.*

Right: *The chandeliers in this view looking west in the long barn were made in Dublin to Patrick Scott's design. The two chandeliers together hold thirty candles. A mid nineteenth-century Irish patchwork quilt hangs on the far wall; red and white designs were particularly popular in the north of Ireland. The 'console' tables are an old pine kitchen table cut in half.*

Above: *Patrick Scott prefers to paint on a flat table surface. One of Ireland's most celebrated artists, his most recent exhibition – 'Windows on the World' in Dublin – followed a period wandering the world. The wall hanging, entitled* Flower of Oaxaca *is from Mexico – a reminder of trips he has made designing for the weavers of Oaxaca.*

doors! These drawings are not representational, but often look like different kinds of foliage. The act of doing them is the important thing – usually I do them to get myself out of a 'block'.

There is an endless round of other work to be done in the country. I make a point of not getting involved in gardening, because that could develop into a full-time passion. I cut the grass, or get help to do so, and I only have one hedge to cut. I have a few naturalized plants like the yellow poppies so hated by serious gardeners, and of course those navy blue columbines. I buy wild flower seeds whenever I see them, and scatter them hopefully. I plant bulbs every year, and they flower well, except for the crocuses which were all eaten by squirrels.

After the reconstruction of the house, money was scarce so I had to find other ways of acquiring furniture. I was given the contents of a derelict cottage in exchange for a couple of watercolours; I found two Victorian metal campaign chairs in a skip; I found a splendid folding metal bed abandoned in a field; and I bought the big dresser in the kitchen and three tables for a pound.

After that initial scavenging, I relaxed and looked around. I have always been interested in vernacular furniture and I started to collect 'famine chairs' or 'fools' stools' as they are sometimes called. I have also collected quite a few old 'sugawn' chairs and items from old dairies.

The big table in the long barn came from the kitchen of a big house in the west of Ireland. It has a reversible top so that I have a clean scrubbed side for parties and a dirty paint-spattered side for working. The top is simply made from four heavy boards bolted together with long bolts, and just sits on the frame. Although most of the objects and furniture are Irish, there are also small things that I have brought home with me from my wanderings around the world: wooden animals and bowls from Mexico, a Japanese *noren* hanging in a low doorway to warn people against banging their heads, and many other pieces that I enjoy having in County Wicklow.

———————— ❧ ————————

When living in the country I enjoy whatever is edible from the hedgerows. In June the flowers of the elderflower can be picked to make elderflower 'champagne'. Mixed with gooseberries the elderflower makes a delicious syrup tasting of muscatel grapes. This can be made into a sorbet, and also is useful for flavouring fruit salads and summer drinks. Here are the recipes.

ELDERFLOWER 'CHAMPAGNE'

700 g (1½ lb) castor or superfine sugar   *30 ml (2 tablespoons) white wine*
4.8 l (1 gallon) cold water   *vinegar*
7–10 heads of elderflower   *juice and rind of 1 lemon*

Put the sugar and water into a big bowl and stir until the sugar is dissolved. Add the remaining ingredients and leave to stand for 24 hours. Strain the liquid into 4 screw-top bottles and leave in a cool place for at least 2 weeks. Cool well before drinking.

Above: *Originally a byre for two dozen cows, the long barn was unheated so during the conversion a fireplace based on a local example was built into the east end and a crane for suspending pots or kettles installed. Old rush light holders and a traditional turf basket stand beside it.*

GOOSEBERRY AND ELDERFLOWER SYRUP

1.8 kg (4 lb) gooseberries, topped and   *600 ml (1 pt/2½ cups) water*
*   tailed*   *12 heads of elderflower*
1.4 kg (3 lb) castor or superfine sugar

Put the sugar and water into a pan. When the sugar is dissolved, add the gooseberries and simmer them gently for 5 to 10 minutes. Add the washed elderflower heads tied in muslin bag or jelly bag and allow to infuse until the syrup is well flavoured. Turn the mixture into a nylon sieve, muslin bag or jelly bag and allow it to drain thoroughly. Strain it again through a piece of muslin or cheesecloth, pour the syrup into bottles and sterilize for 10 minutes. (The latter need only be done if the syrup is to be kept for some months. There is no need to sterilize if it is going to be used within 4 weeks.) The fruit pulp left over from this recipe can be used in a gooseberry fool.

Some years ago, I found a place where chanterelles appear every August, and I consider myself to be very lucky. This year there was a bumper crop. I was away for the early part of August, and when I finally got to the place, I was blinded by the quantities of apricot caps shining through the rough grass. I had fortunately brought a large plastic bag, and I filled it. I gave half of them away to a friend. She asked me to lunch, served them with sweetbreads, and they were delicious.

Above: *The kitchen was converted from the old stables and half of the old loft floor was replaced by a balcony, now used for sleeping as it probably was before. Old Irish earthenware jugs and dairy crocks line the edge of the balcony. The glazed door leading outside from the kitchen faces east with a view up the hill.*

133

Above: *In August chanterelle mushrooms grow in profusion in certain hidden places around Ballynabrocky. They are delicious cooked with cream and eaten with eggs or sweetbreads or sautéed on their own and served on a piece of buttered bread. This simple meal would be finished to perfection by a dish of wild strawberries; these are also found in the woods and hedgerows nearby.*

Usually I only find a couple of handfuls at a time, so I cook them with cream and serve them with eggs, for example with soft-boiled eggs as a sauce. Or I use them as a filling for an omelette, or indeed add them to scrambled eggs during the cooking. They are also wonderful served simply on a piece of buttered toast.

If I was serving chanterelles with meat, I would sweat a couple of shallots, chopped, in the pan before adding the chanterelles and maybe a crushed clove of garlic.

CHANTERELLES A LA CREME

225 g (8 oz) chanterelles
50 g (2 oz/$\frac{1}{4}$ cup) butter
45–60 ml (3–4 tablespoons) double or heavy cream

salt and pepper
pinch chopped parsley

Clean the chanterelles and cut off the earthy part of stem. Slice the stem thinly across – this is because the stem is tougher than the cap, which can be left whole or roughly chopped. Melt the nob of butter in a pan, then add the chopped chanterelles and cook for about 5 minutes; they give off quite a lot of moisture, but this will quickly evaporate. Add the cream, and cook for a few more minutes, then season to taste and sprinkle with chopped parsley.

Left: *The canopied bed in the main bedroom, now made up with an Irish patchwork quilt, was found on the roadside. The walls were washed with a lime and water mixture and the floor covered in woven rush matting. The circular painting on the wall by Patrick Scott is 'for meditation'.*

Top: *Rush light holders, a weaver bird's nest from Zimbabwe and other mementoes decorate the window board and a scrubbed pine table in the old kitchen. Rush lights were made by half peeling the skin from a rush and soaking the pith in oil or lard.*

Above: *Lough Tay at Luggala is a spectacular lake set within a granite horseshoe about five miles from Ballynabrocky. The stream that meanders down from the mountains in the distance supplies the lake with rich fresh peaty water.*

MR GEORGE STACPOOLE

BALLYNACOURTY
County Limerick

When we got married some twenty years ago, our first task was to find a house in which to live. As with most newly married couples, our budget was limited. We professed a preference for an area in west Limerick because of its proximity to where we worked. My wife, Michelina, designs knitwear, and I am involved with antiques and the antiquarian and second-hand book business.

We searched every by-road looking for a suitable house. At last we found Ballynacourty. The owners of the property had left it many years previously, and so it had become almost totally derelict. Cows walked through the house, windows were broken, and there were briars everywhere. We made a deal with the owners on the site, agreeing to purchase the house and grounds for £3000. At the time we never thought of asking them to indicate to us the boundaries of the property and, to our great surprise and delight, our solicitor informed us that as well as the house, we had purchased nine acres of the surrounding land.

The house consisted of two rooms on the ground floor, and three rooms upstairs. There was also a long, single-storeyed room at the front of the house, and a collapsing wing at the back. This latter we immediately demolished. So we had a sound basic structure with which to work. We enlisted the help of an architect friend, Paddy Leyden, to help us in our task of making the house habitable. The plans were drawn up, and we found a superb local builder, Stephen Clancy. We owe much of the development of the property over the years to his ideas and work. He has seen us through every change, both with and without an architect.

Initially we enlarged all the windows and put in more windows because it is so important to take advantage of light, and particularly

Above: *Peppers, courgettes, avocados, beans, tomatoes, potatoes, peaches and nectarines . . . these are the base ingredients from which Michelina Stacpoole – 'the best cook in the county' – will prepare luncheon.*

Opposite, left: *When it was installed, the Aga cooker in the kitchen cost just about the same amount of money that was paid for the entire house fifteen years earlier, but it has proved its worth as a source of year-round warmth in a room that has become the heart of the house. A collection of blue and white plates and strainers is displayed on the wall above, along with an Irish eighteenth-century toasting fork.*

Previous page: *One of two Irish pine dressers in the kitchen, this one displays a collection of blue and white china of Oriental design, including some Nankin plates, as well as the usual accoutrements of an accomplished cook. Old tea tins are ranged along the top of the dresser.*

sunshine, in our Irish climate. In place of the demolished wing we built a large kitchen downstairs and, above it, a room which became our bedroom. This room has superb views of the river Shannon and in the distance, on the other side of the river, we can just see the international Shannon airport.

We decided on a large kitchen as we knew we would spend many hours there, and also we wanted a room where we could entertain informally. We put terracotta tiles on the floor and had special pine cupboards made by a local joiner. He had never before made anything of this nature. We showed him what we wanted and how to achieve it, and from that beginning he developed a prosperous business in kitchen units! Our kitchen table is pine, large and round with well-worn legs. The previous owners had cats who had obviously used the legs for sharpening their claws. We have two Irish pine dressers displaying a collection of blue and white plates. On the walls we have our collection of nineteenth-century china strainers, from various potteries.

Some five years ago we decided to install an Aga cooker. This cost us exactly the same amount of money that we had paid for the house and land some fifteen years earlier. It was worth it because not only do the entire family appreciate the Aga, but so do the dogs, Pupa and Tosca, especially in winter months when they spend all day huddled against it.

The two original downstairs rooms of the house are now our dining room and small drawing room. The dining room leads off the new kitchen; in fact it was the original kitchen of the house. We put two extra windows in the dining room, and in doing so had to knock through a wall some three feet thick. On one wall we have a fitted bookcase full of books and decorative china and glass, including an old wine bottle which reminds us of an ancestor's good living. It has the seal of James Stacpoole and is dated 1714. James lived at Mountcashel, in County Clare. The house stands on the edge of a lake, and this bottle was found on the bottom of the lake several years ago, perhaps thrown out after some wild party.

Another favourite piece that we keep in the dining room is a reminder of days when recipients of kind deeds were very appreciative. It is a chinoiserie silver basket that has come into my possession by descent through the family. It has the following inscription:

Mrs Jane Browne of Newgrove in the County of Clare and Kingdom of Ireland, in acknowledgement of her careful and tender and affectionate behaviour to an Orphan Child William Miller ever mindful of the motherly regard he stood so much in need of takes leave to offer this memorial of her humanity and his gratitude London May 5th 1755.

We use this basket every day for fruit and cakes.

We both love pictures and throughout the house every wall is covered in them. The dining room is no exception; it has many eighteenth- and nineteenth-century topographical views of the surrounding area, which we collect.

Top: *This view from the driveway illustrates the south front of the house and the adjoining guest wing. The single-storeyed room at the front, part of which is original, is the entrance hall and, with so many windows, one of the sunniest rooms in the house.*

Above: *The guest bedroom is sumptuously furnished with an elegant four-poster bed, hung with a gathered pelmet in a fabric that matches the pelmets beneath the gilded crenated boards at the windows. The bedside table is nineteenth-century Irish. Richard John Stacpoole, the grandfather of the present owner, painted the watercolours on the wall.*

The small drawing room is the room we use as a family room. As its name implies, it is small and cosy and has a marble mantelpiece with a delightful centre plaque of a boy with a horse and plough. Our sofa and chairs are covered in a highly impractical white fabric, with lots of patchwork and needlepoint cushions scattered about. The dogs love these cushions. They snuggle down on them and, as this is a family room, no harsh words are spoken. Books pile up everywhere, and on various small tables there are collections of boxes made in different materials. The walls are covered in pictures. A favourite is called *The Eventful Consultation* by Nicholas Crowley, RHA. It depicts a family grouped around a girl who is having her pulse taken. There are pieces of jewellery and musical instruments everywhere, but nothing to indicate what has happened to the girl or the reason for her pulse being taken. It is the subject of endless speculation.

The long room at the front of the house, part of which was original to the house, is our entrance hall. It has many windows and faces south, so in the early part of the day, it is wonderful to sit here, enjoy the sunshine and perhaps read the newspapers. As this room did not go the full length of the house, we added a room which now is a tiny study filled with books. The other end links the house with the wing we built in 1973 when my father was going to come and live with us. He required a large drawing room to take his favourite pieces of furniture, plus a bedroom and a bathroom. Sadly he died some weeks before he was due to move in. Some of those favourite pieces are now in the house, including a tall grandfather clock in a fine mahogany case made by the estate carpenter to my grandfather who lived in Eden Vale near Ennis, County Clare. In the bedroom, which has a four-poster bed, the walls are covered in watercolours painted by my grandfather Richard John Stacpoole, who was a gifted amateur. We have drawings and watercolours executed by various members of the family in the past century throughout the house.

The drawing room has a reasonable formality about it. One cabinet is full of china by James Donovan of Dublin who decorated pieces from the late eighteenth century into the early part of the nineteenth century. We have tried to collect as much of this rare china as possible, and have pieces painted with views of Dublin, botanical scenes, birds and mythology. He was given the name 'The Emperor of China', which he well deserved. Over the mantelpiece hangs a nineteenth-century American primitive portrait of two sisters. We bought this at a sale for eleven pounds. On another wall hangs a portrait of Great Aunt Fat and Great Aunt Gwen delightfully painted by St George Hare. Across the room hangs a picture of ourselves and the children painted by Thomas Ryan, PRHA, painted so that future generations can see how we were. Like so many things in the house, we collected the pictures because we liked them; others we were lucky enough to inherit.

Upstairs there are three bedrooms. Hassard and Sebastian, our sons, have walls covered in blue and white gingham. Again, pictures abound in this room, especially ones related to Irish railways as this is Hassard's passion. Frederick Stacpoole was a nineteenth-century engraver of some importance. We collect his engravings and a favourite, entitled *Worn Out*, hangs in the boys' room. It shows an old man sleeping in a chair

Above: *The large drawing room houses a great variety of pictures as well as interesting pieces of china and other artefacts. The room achieves the combination of formality and comfort that epitomizes country-house style.*

Right: *The long south-facing hall connects the reception rooms on the ground floor. It houses an eighteenth-century black lacquer cabinet displaying a mixture of Delft and blue and white Chinese porcelain. On the other side of the door to the small drawing room, there is a carved gilt Irish table, also from the eighteenth century.*

Left: *This picture shows a detail of a silver cake basket of chinoiserie design, made in London in 1746. It is inscribed to 'Mrs Jane Browne of Newgrove in the County of Clare' for her 'tender and affectionate behaviour to an orphan child'.*

beside a child in a bed; a mouse runs around his feet. On the opposite side of the landing, the spare room is full of watercolours of local interest including the interior of a tent of an army officer, drawn near Limerick in 1832. It shows what incredible comfort the officers lived in in those days.

Our own bedroom is dominated by the four-poster bed and the wonderful view of the river.

Two years ago we made the best addition to the house when we built a conservatory. One day, travelling near Limerick we saw some windows which looked to have been abandoned. Upon enquiry we found the owner and bought them from him for £100. Together with some glass doors we found in Dublin, the windows formed the basis of the conservatory. Living in Ireland's unpredictable climate, we find it the perfect solution. We use it for entertaining during the summer months, and at times throughout the year we sit there and enjoy it.

The house looks deceptively small from the outside, and people are always amazed at its size when they venture indoors. The sense of space is in part due to the fact that the rooms link with one another, and there is no space given over to passages; also there is no hidden servants' wing. We run the house with the help of Margaret Madigan who has been with us for many years. She helped look after the boys when they were small. She is a very important part of our lives as, with Michelina and me having careers outside the house, our lifestyle tends to be rather hectic. It is at the weekends that the house comes into its own.

Michelina loves to cook. She says it is a relaxation, and indeed she reads a cookbook as eagerly as she reads a novel. We always seem to have people coming for meals. We like to share with other people the pleasure we ourselves derive from the house. My greatest relaxation is the garden which, like the house, we have developed over the years. We converted two fields into a two-acre garden which makes the house look as though it has been a part of the landscape for generations.

We have been here for twenty years and nearly every year we have made some alteration or addition to the house. At the end of each year we say we are finished, we will do no more, but somehow we always find something more to do. How boring it would be to live in a place that was perfect – thank goodness we do not!

Above: *The cup and saucer illustrated are by James Donovan who worked from the late eighteenth century into the early nineteenth. With its green scale background and delicate insets it illustrates the high standard of gilding and hand-painting he achieved. Made c. 1810, it is signed and dated in script in black: Donovan, Dublin.*

Below: *Luncheon dishes, including Pollo alla Cacciatore Con Pomodori (see the recipe on this page), aubergines, beans and potatoes, are displayed on the round antique pine table in the kitchen before being taken through to the conservatory.*

We have served these dishes to friends in the past, and they always seem to go down well. The Avocado Pear Mould looks attractive and the chicken dish requires very little time to prepare.

AVOCADO PEAR MOULD

15 g (½ oz/2 envelopes) gelatine
30 ml (2 tablespoons) water
10 ml (2 teaspoons) lemon juice
150 ml (5 fl oz) chicken stock
2 avocados
10 ml (2 teaspoons) Worcester sauce

10 g (2 heaping teaspoons) mild curry powder
150 ml (5 fl oz) double or heavy cream
150 ml (5 fl oz) mayonnaise (home-made)
salt and pepper

FOR THE FILLING

150 ml (5 fl oz) mayonnaise
5 g (1 heaping teaspoon) mild curry powder

100 g (4 oz) prawns, cooked and peeled

Serves 6

Melt the gelatine in the water and the lemon juice over a gentle heat. Add the chicken stock and leave to cool. Peel the avocados and remove the stones, then mash the flesh of the avocado. Now add the gelatine stock, the Worcester sauce and the curry powder and leave until almost set. Whip the cream until stiff, and fold the whipped cream and the mayonnaise into the avocado mixture. Season to taste. Now damp a ring mould with cold water. Spoon in the mixture and leave in a refrigerator to set, covered with cling film or plastic wrap.

For the filling, prepare some home-made mayonnaise and add the curry and the prawns. Turn out the mould on a platter and fill it with the prawn mixture. You may of course fill the mould with a mixture of your choice, perhaps a different shellfish or an egg mixture.

This main course is excellent with a crisp salad and a gratin dauphinois.

POLLO ALLA CACCIATORE CON POMODORI

30 ml (2 large tablespoons) olive oil
½ onion, chopped
parsley, chopped
celery, chopped
1 clove garlic, chopped
1 chicken (large), cut into pieces

1 bay leaf
½ glass white wine
1 can tomatoes
salt and pepper
chopped parsley, to garnish

Serves 6

Preheat the oven to 180°C (350°F, gas mark 4).

Take a large flame-proof casserole dish and put in it the olive oil, chopped onion, parsley, celery and garlic. Sauté for a few minutes before putting in the pieces of chicken. Let it all sauté gently until everything is a pale gold colour. Now put in the bay leaf. Continue to sauté until dark gold in colour. At this point add the wine, and simmer the dish to let it evaporate. Then put in the tomatoes. Season to taste. Stir the dish, then cover it and put it in the oven for about 30 minutes or until cooked. Serve on a platter garnished with a little chopped parsley.

BLACKCURRANT PUDDING

1.2 kg (2½ lb) blackcurrants
sugar to taste

600 ml (1 pt/2½ cups) double or *heavy cream*

Serves 6

Stew the blackcurrants with the sugar for a few hours, then mouli the mixture (do not liquidize). Let it cool, then whip the cream and fold it into the blackcurrants. Put the mixture in a glass bowl and leave in the fridge overnight before serving.

Left: *The conservatory on the west side is a new addition to the house. Constructed from some windows found abandoned on a road near Limerick, together with glass doors from Dublin, a lovely light room has been created that allows the Stacpooles to cater for the vagaries of Irish weather. They entertain in the conservatory in the summer and on sunny days in the winter.*

Above: *In a corner of the conservatory, a nineteenth-century bust does dual service as an ornament and a hat-stand between a pair of nineteenth-century church candlesticks.*

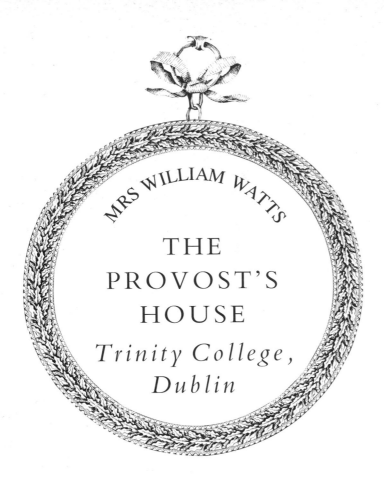

MRS WILLIAM WATTS

THE PROVOST'S HOUSE
Trinity College, Dublin

I f you marry a curate you may hope to live in a bishop's palace. If you marry a third secretary then an embassy in a foreign country could be your goal. However, when I married a fellow student I did not expect to move into the Provost's House some thirty years later. In my own time as a student the provost seemed to me a remote figure whose existence was only brought to my notice when lectures were cancelled because of his death. In those days the house, too, was remote, its big gates on Grafton Street closed and cut off from the college, as we students knew it, by the Fellows' Garden. Nowadays the arts building overlooks the Provost's Garden, students chain their bicycles to the back gate and tourists knock on the front door to enquire for the Book of Kells, so we feel very much part of college life.

Inside the house things are different, too. In the 1930s there were at least five indoor staff but now there is only one full-time man, the provost's steward, who does everything from answering the door and serving drinks to scrubbing the flagged floors and carrying out the rubbish. He is helped by two women whose morning's work includes polishing acres of antique tables and innumerable brass fittings. The rooms in the basement have keys whose labels still say 'Housekeeper's room' and 'Kitchenmaid's room', but they are now used either as family bedrooms or as picture stores. Needless to say, because we have to be security conscious, the keys we use every day look a little different to these standard Victorian ones, and getting into the Provost's House is rather like getting into Fort Knox.

The Provost's House is the only one of the great Georgian stone houses which is still used for its original purpose. Since 1760, provosts and their families have lived here. This gives the house a comfortable, lived-in

Above: *This photograph shows a bust of Emperor Caracalla, set on a gold wall bracket at the north end of the saloon.*

Previous page: *The intricate wrought-iron balustrade and lavish plasterwork embellishing the oval light in the ceiling above the entrance to the saloon, are typical of the rich decorative work visible throughout the Provost's House. (The lobby light is itself a typical feature of Irish country houses.) Just as the arches and cornicing of the lobby are repeated in the upper landing, so the plasterwork rectangle in a Greek key design and the inner arabesques are echoed in the ceiling above.*

feeling and if there are any ghosts they are pleasant cheerful ones. Lack of staff has meant, however, that usage of the rooms has recently changed. The large dining room, the drawing room and the beautiful saloon are only used for formal occasions and the family lives in private rooms at the top of the house, in the basement and in the south wing. We have had to spread ourselves throughout the house in this way as making a dining room, sitting room and study for everyday use upstairs left the house with only two bedrooms. As we had a son and a daughter living with us when we moved in, we had to accommodate them in the basement.

There are eighty-three stone steps spiralling up from the basement to our living area so it was necessary to work out ways of communicating that did not cause utter exhaustion. My daughter and I fixed up a pulley with a bag and a bell so that, if I wish to attract her attention when I am upstairs, I can pull on the bell and she will come to the foot of the stairs. I can then ask her to put the milk or whatever I have forgotten into the bag and haul it up. She has also devised an indicator board so that we know whether she is in or out for the phone or a friend. On the ground floor, we have converted the pleasant garden room into a small sitting room

Left: *The coffered ceiling, corinthian columns, pediments and arches in the saloon are highly decorative. The room is a fine example of the way the architectural precepts of ancient Greece and Rome were adopted and embellished in the great classical revival of the eighteenth century. The plasterwork was achieved by the Wall brothers of Dublin.*

Above: *A portrait of the foundress of the college, Queen Elizabeth I, resplendent in ruff and jewels, hangs within a decorative panel in the saloon.*

which is convenient for day-time use with its access to the garden and its proximity to the front door and the telephone.

It is impossible to live in an historic institution without developing an interest in earlier residents. The spirit of Francis Andrews who had the house built is felt everywhere in the grand design of the hall and staircase, and in the magnificent saloon which extends the whole length of the house and into two storeys. His portrait hangs at one end of this room, and his beautifully embroidered waistcoat and the splendid fall of lace at his collar and cuffs complement the richness of the plasterwork on the cornice and the ceiling. He was known as Don Francisco Bumperoso and is alleged to have died of entertaining and being entertained. At the other end of the saloon hangs a portrait of the 4th Duke of Bedford who was chancellor of the university when Andrews was provost. Dressed in scarlet, his chest laden with orders and decorations and his leg placed so that part of the motto of the Knights of the Garter – 'Honi soit qui mal y pense' (Evil he who evil thinks) – can be read, he looks as if he, too, enjoyed the good things of life. Portraits of two of the college founders also hang in the saloon: Queen Elizabeth I, severe in face but resplendent in lace and pearls, who founded the College of the Holy and Undivided

Above: *A favourite lithograph, by J. W. Morrison, entitled* Dublin in 1776, *hangs in the garden room. It illustrates Grafton Street and the Provost's House and various individuals have been named beneath. The street was as full of life then as it is now.*

Right: *The dining room, again beautifully decorative, the plasterwork standing out against the terracotta-coloured walls, contains two good portraits (one of Edmund Burke by James Barry and the other of Samuel Maddon) and also this picture by Pieter Lastman –* Coreolanus Receiving the Envoys *– which was painted in 1625.*

Trinity near Dublin in 1592, and James Ussher, very much the scholar in appearance, who collected classical manuscripts to form our earliest library. In the early seventeenth century he was famous for working out from biblical references that the world was created in 4004 BC – a date which was accepted by believers for the next 250 years.

The small dining room contains James Barry's portrait of Burke and, more important for the house, a large portrait of Samuel Madden, who left his valuable collection of paintings to be displayed here. Although he was Provost Andrews' friend, he looks quite a different character. He chose to be painted informally wearing a velvet cap instead of an elaborate wig and dressed in the simple black of an Anglican minister. Even the Geneva bands at his neck are slightly tossed to one side and he is looking up from what is obviously a prayer book or devotional work.

The library is very much a working room with college committee meetings held there at least once a week, watched over by several earlier provosts. John Hely-Hutchinson, who had the library built onto the north wing when he followed Francis Andrews as provost, looks down from one wall, while my personal favourite, Provost Salmon, smiles with gentle but wry humour from above the door.

Above: *The window ledge on the stairs down to the basement, just off the main entrance hall, displays a blackboard with an indicator to show whether members of the family who live downstairs are in or out. Thus, when the telephone or doorbell rings for them, unnecessary journeys to find them can be avoided.*

All these portraits give a wonderful sense of continuity and community, and there is one piece of furniture which links us back with an earlier foundation. When Queen Elizabeth established the college she gave it land which had been sequestered in her father's time from the Monastery of All Hallows. The medieval monks had grown mulberry trees in their garden and old inventories and plans show that some of these trees lasted on in the Provost's Garden until 1850. Then, in a violent storm on the night of 18 April, the last mulberry tree was blown down and Richard McDonnell, who was then provost, had the wood made into the marquetry top for a small table which still sits in our drawing room.

I have talked about the portraits of the Provost's House rather than its architecture because it is the people who have lived and visited here as part of the community of Fellows and Scholars of Trinity College who bring the house alive for me. An institutional residence could easily become an impersonal museum. That it has not done so is a tribute to all those who have lived in it over the last 227 years. Living here has been an honour, a challenge and a responsibility, but it has also been a pleasure. I will finish by describing one last picture which hangs in our garden room. It is entitled *Dublin in 1776* and shows Grafton Street and the

Provost's House. A coach drawn by four horses is coming out of the gates of the Provost's House and the street outside is full of life. Lady Clare, Lady Caher and Lady Denny are talking to the Duke of Leinster and Lord Henry Fitzgerald while Lady Louisa and Squire Conolly ride past. (The names are given underneath.) In the wall of the Provost's House is a cobbler's hut with the cobbler doing business and the Wicklow sandman is carrying his wares past a notice for a play in the Smock Alley Theatre. When I look at this picture I feel the strength of both continuity and community. The Provost's House is still in the centre of Dublin and is now, with the breaking down of class barriers to university entrance, even more at the centre of Dublin life.

Like most people with even a drop of Scottish blood, ginger and treacle are two of my favourite flavours and these two recipes contain both.

GINGERBREAD

450 g (1 lb) flour
7 ml (1½ heaping teaspoons) finely grated ginger
10 ml (2 heaping teaspoons) baking powder
3 ml (½ heaping teaspoon) baking soda
pinch salt

225 g (8 oz/1⅓ cups) brown sugar
175 g (6 oz/¾ cup) margarine
225 g (8 oz/¾ cup) treacle or blackstrap molasses
275 ml (10 fl oz) milk
1 egg, beaten

Preheat the oven to 180°C (350°F, gas mark 4).

Sieve together the flour, ginger, baking powder, baking soda and salt. Set aside. Over a low heat, mix the sugar, margarine, treacle *or* molasses and milk, stirring constantly. When they are completely melted, stir in the beaten egg and fold in the dry ingredients. Pour the mixture into a greased, lined tin or pan and bake for 1½ hours. Cool on a wire rack and serve cut into slices and buttered.

TREACLE BISCUITS

These are very easy and great fun for children to make.

175 g (6 oz/¾ cup) margarine
100 g (4 oz/½ cup) sugar
1 egg
30 ml (2 tablespoons) treacle or blackstrap molasses
225 g (8 oz/1½ cups) flour

5 ml (1 heaping teaspoon) baking soda
pinch salt
5 ml (1 heaping teaspoon) ground cinnamon
5 ml (1 heaping teaspoon) ground cloves
5 ml (1 heaping teaspoon) ground ginger

Preheat the oven to about 230°C (450°F, gas mark 8).

Put into a blender and beat together the margarine, sugar, egg and treacle *or* molasses. Then, using a knife, fold in the flour, baking soda, and salt. Sieve the spices together and add them to the mixture. Shape the mixture into walnut-sized pieces and bake on a well-greased tray for 10 minutes. Cool on a wire rack.

Left: *The staircase hall, with its delicate ironwork balustrade and emphatic stonework, displays a portrait of Bishop Butler within a carved oak frame. Just visible on the left of the picture is the corner of a splendid staircase window; arched and pedimented, it dominates the staircase hall and fills it with light.*

Top: *The college dining hall, on the other side of the quadrangle to the Provost's House, was recently gutted by fire but has now been restored. It has been laid for a special commemorative dinner with silver candlesticks, Irish potato rings and menu cards. 'Commons' is served in this hall every evening for resident students and academics.*

Above: *Begun in 1759, perhaps by Henry Keene or John Smyth, the Provost's House is almost a direct copy of the house Lord Burlington designed in 1723 for General Wade in London, which in turn was derived from an original Palladio drawing owned by Burlington.*

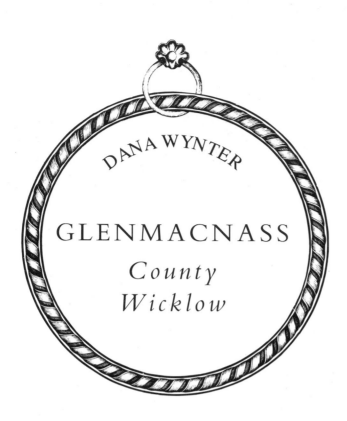

DANA WYNTER

GLENMACNASS
*County
Wicklow*

I was sent to Ireland from America on a professional assignment. We worked six days a week and the usual twelve-hour day and my driver, good Irishman that he is, was pained by the fact that his country was not receiving its due appreciation and determined to correct the omission. From the moment I was bundled into the car and driven off into the rain that Sunday morning my fate, as they say, was sealed – even though six years were to pass before I realized it.

The narrow road from Dublin over the Featherbed Mountains curved through wide stretches of peat-bog dusted with pink heather and white bog-cotton. Thousands of truffle-brown sods of turf, cut and stacked to dry in the sun and wind, stood silhouetted like small dolmens against the changing sky. It was a long lonely road, a circling hawk and mountain sheep the only sign of a living presence. The road seemed to be lost in the folds of the hills – until a turn skirted the top of a 350-foot waterfall to reveal what I now know is one of the most beautiful glens in Ireland.

There was a burst of sunlight and then, quite as suddenly, the valley was wrapped in a veil of water vapour, and vanished. We drove on through one winding leafy road after another, braving warnings – 'BEWARE DANGEROUS BRIDGE' – which in the event were no more than small hump-back bridges, past farmhouses offering strawberries, raspberries, and something mysterious called 'pinks' which turned out to be not plants but potatoes . . . and back to Dublin. The memory of the magical glen stayed with me but dimmed in the skein of dislocated impressions and capricious weather.

Years passed and the longing for a tiny house in the Irish countryside became overwhelming, so I made an appointment to see a thatched

Above: *The sitting room, with its plain whitewashed walls, is both rustic and minimal in effect. The fireplace boasts an Irish country cooking crane which is in daily use. It swings over the flames to support kettles and pans while they heat. The whaling kettle with its large round base, is from Maine in the United States. A cottage chair from the west of Ireland stands before the hearth.*

Above right: *A variety of objects from different ages and cultures are displayed on the shelves by the fireplace; these include Nautilus shells, a Yucatan clay whistle, a pre-Colombian statue of a man and a dog, an Irish penal cross, a clay cup from the wreck of a seventeenth-century Spanish galleon, a Mexican clay whistle, bamboo coral from Hawaii, a Russian battle icon, African snuff bottles and pots, and Ashanti gold weights.*

Previous page: *The bedroom enjoys glorious views northeast towards the waterfall. It is furnished very simply, in keeping with the rest of the house, and the objects of interest stand out against the bare walls. The wooden man on the right of the picture is Indian while the spinning wheel is Irish and in constant use. A basket of teased, carded Wicklow fleece stands before it.*

cottage which was for sale in County Wicklow. The local grocer (impressive in the suit saved for weddings, funerals, and real estate transactions) and I sat in the pub in Roundwood gloomily watching the rain come down in stair-rods as the Irish say ('in fleece' is the country term) awaiting the owner who was to be an hour late due to an unfortunate collision with a sheep on the road en route.

'Well, why not go up and see some land that's for sale?'

'There's no point, I live in America, I couldn't possibly build a house from that distance.'

'Better than sitting here, seeing as how neither one of us drinks.'

'Oh all RIGHT,' I agreed, somewhat ungraciously.

We set off in Mr Curley's car, the rain doubled its efforts, the windscreen-wipers packed up and I stonily tried to avert thoughts of sunny California. Then a gate loomed through the mists and further investigation showed the outline of a path leading down to the remains of a ruined chimney. There was a sound of falling water. Suddenly the rain slackened, the sun burst through the clouds and I was standing in the middle of the valley I'd never thought to find again. The waterfall was almost a stone's throw away. *Sa chiuint* ... fate ... kismet ... it was written.

So the house was built of local granite by our farmer-builder neighbour, on a handshake. Long oaten straw for the roof was grown in Roundwood two villages away (now we have sturdy Wicklow reed, but that's another story). My son and I spend every moment we can here, willingly drawn into the gentle side of life, the rhythm of the seasons and above all, country priorities.

The year unfolds with a series of surprises. We open the shutters each morning to look at the waterfall which sets the mood of the day; often in full spate, sometimes she veils her head to dream, brood or sulk and hide the place where the rocks make a step to form a pool which often mirrors the setting sun – the water seems on fire, molten, and the mind wanders to the possibility that water might be liquid light.

Rosy evening skies indicate a good day to follow. If there have been gales during the night – our bad weather comes from the north east and funnels down the valley with surprising ferocity – then all the plants must be lifted from the ground *again* and retied to the walls. When ravenous sheep come thundering over the cattle grid, then its on with the wellies to chase them out without earning a heart-attack in the process. When snows bring normal life to a halt it's time to take out the typewriter and open the folder of work left mouldering under the heading of 'Later'. Better still, we walk up to the waterfall for the joy of seeing the faintest trace of a small bird's feet and tail-feather etching his passing on new snow. And with luck the sides of the valley are hung with ribbons and ropes of frozen falling water shimmering in cool sunlight. Spinneys mark the glen with cold branches bearing bouquets of black birds. At home Finbarr, the haughty pheasant who graciously adopted us three years ago, becomes even more tyrannical about the punctuality of his breakfast, having breasted his way through the snow to get it like the figurehead of a ship, all moving parts totally obscured. A moment's tardiness on our part brings him up onto a sill to hammer at the window with his beak.

Suddenly it's spring. The light changes and larches stand in a faint pale green haze of new growth, herons mark small brown trout in the stream with a beady eye, ewes and twin lambs live under our windows and the car is free of its crystal casket of ice for another year. Crocuses give way to narcissi and daffodils, ferns uncurl in the crevices of pale grey granite walls. Badgers and the occasional fox wander the glen roads at night, both unaware of the hostility and murderous intent of the farming community. There are drifts of confetti when May blossoms mark the beginning of the season, then speckled foxgloves glaze the landscape pink while honeysuckle and dog-roses fill the hedges. Raindrops transform a slim twig into a Lalique centipede. Five deer come down from the forest to cross the stream and recently their young fawn timidly stretched its neck to touch noses with a new lamb in the field by our front door. We wonder where the kestrels will nest this year.

In summer the fields are soft with ferns and there's a scent of honey in the air. Nights have the luminous sheen of endless twilight and my son fishes until the early hours of the morning. We wait for the moon to be full each month and celebrate by accompanying our shadows up to the waterfall to look down onto this valley carved 10,000 years ago by glaciers and illuminated now as then, by palest white light.

Then in autumn the glen becomes foxed like the leaves of an old book. There are blackberries in the hedges and sloes waiting for the first bloom of frost before they are harvested for essential sloe-gin; rowan berries are picked for delicate pink jelly to accompany venison and elderberry flowers and fruit also go into the cooking. Squirrels and birds tend to be winners in the race for hazelnuts, but then fair's fair. There's a winding down of the year: sheep have long been shorn, feathery bracken turns

Top: *From the top of the Glenmacnass waterfall – a 'stone's throw' away from the cottage – this is the view of the valley. Carved 10,000 years ago by glaciers, the valley floor is farmed but the hillsides accommodate only sheep. The sixth-century monastery, Glendalough, is hidden to the west, and can be reached by walking down the valley and then up over the hills to the right.*

Above: *Dana Wynter stands outside the entrance door of the cottage, which was built for her a few years ago in local granite. The roof is thatched in Wicklow river-reed. The climbing rose is 'Galway Bay', the clematis is of the Montana variety, and geraniums, wild poppies, pansies, strawberry plants and various herbs are ranged in pots and beds around the steps.*

sanguine-red and our glen road becomes edged with yellow where the forest larches drop their needles.

And we walk. Four miles away monastic sixth-century Glendalough sleeps in a nest of antiquity beside her two lakes guarded by granite hills. Nearby St Kevin's bed – a cleft in a rock high above the dark Upper Lake – was a Bronze Age tomb. An overgrown path meanders past the high Round Tower and random headstones tilted and mossed, some worn smooth as a bishop's ring, mark the centuries with inscriptions like the distillation of a Wicklow man's character as defined by 'his disconsolate widow':

LUKE O'TOOLE 1785
He was ever a comfort to the distressed
Father to the orphaned
His door ever opened to the poor

Further on, past the forest skirting the lake's upper reaches, we arrive in a strange lunar landscape with old disused lead mines and novice Alpinists hanging on ropes from inhospitable rock-face. Once over the crown of the mountain we are back in our own valley.

When the house was finished a formal garden seemed out of place, an intrusion, so we decided to grow plants which were sympathetic to the district and which would blend naturally into the glen. Anyway, at 900 feet with frequent savage north-east winds, horticultural choice is limited and experiments often heartbreaking. We chose colours which complement native granite and stayed with pale pink roses ('Albertine' is a courageous, generous friend under the worst circumstances), lots of lavender, clematis, pink mallow (lavetera), honeysuckle and, of course, the perfumed philadelphus to remind us of California and orange-groves. Friends from over the mountain gave us rampaging fraises de bois along with some energetic pale green hops for a corner of the house. Bright yellow Welsh poppies have adopted us and that's just fine; other people dismiss them as weeds but we're grateful for anything which flowers profusely and these bloom with the enthusiasm of a World Cup football crowd. Other yellow plants pierce the mists: broom, yellow jasmine and coreopsis.

Ireland, for me, is symbolized by the moon-bow which I have seen only once, during a drive very late one clear night when there were fine traces of water in the air and the moon, full and low in the sky on one side of the country road, threw a wide pale arc over the Djouce Mountains on the other ... Luna, worshipped in pre-Christian times as the White Goddess. Granite is now known to possess measurable radioactivity which peaks at dawn and dusk, but how this is generated and renewed is still a mystery. Perhaps it was our fate to step onto that path linking the ancient Druids through myth and legend to the future.

Sa chiuint.

Top: *Amongst various pies and cakes set on the kitchen table, a plate of chocolate cookies, including Wicklow Brownies (see the recipe on the opposite page), is decorated with 'Albertine' roses from the garden.*

Above: *The shutters are opened every morning for a view of the waterfall which sets the mood of the day. 'Often in full spate, sometimes she veils her head to dream, brood or sulk and hide the place where the rocks make a step to form a pool ...'*

Life inside the house is excessively plain and we live without staff. I have never had the talent or the patience for cooking and firmly pin the blame on the doll-sized stove which accommodates one item at a time and was bought sixteen years ago (a temporary expedient) at the local post office. Visitors are given supportive drinks, then prudently taken to our excellent Roundwood Inn where this whole saga began. Picnics are for tried and true friends. Mercifully, and to their great relief, Ireland produces perfect smoked salmon, trout, and whiskey-salami along with increasing numbers of excellent local cheeses. For chums who come to tea I've learned to bake tolerable bread, traditional Irish brack, oatmeal biscuits (cookies) and brownies. Here are two recipes.

WICKLOW BRACK

350 g (12 oz/2 cups) sultanas or *seedless raisins*

200 g (7 oz/1 cup) soft brown sugar

275 ml (10 fl oz) cold strong tea

1 egg

275 g (10 oz/2 cups) self-raising flour

Preheat the oven to 180°C (350°F, gas mark 4).

Soak the sultanas *or* raisins and sugar in the tea overnight. Stir in the egg and flour using a metal spoon – why I don't know. Bake in 20 cm (8 inch) greased tin or pan for 1¼ hours. Cool on a wire rack before cutting into slices.

WICKLOW BROWNIES

350 g (12 oz) plain or *semi-sweet chocolate*

225 g (8 oz/1 cup) unsalted butter

200 g (7 oz/1 cup) sugar

4 eggs

5 ml (1 teaspoon) vanilla essence or *extract*

150 g (5 oz/1 cup) cake flour

5 ml (1 level teaspoon) baking powder

Preheat the oven to 220°C (425°F, gas mark 7).

Melt the chocolate and butter together in a bain-marie, then allow to cool. Beat together the sugar and the eggs, adding them one at a time. Add the chocolate-butter mixture and vanilla to the eggs and sugar. Sift the flour and baking powder and add them to the mixture. Blend, turning the blender on and off only three times or so. Do not overbeat. Pour the mixture into a shallow greased tin and bake for exactly 20 minutes. Cool for several hours on a wire rack before cutting.

Left, top: *The kitchen is set for lunch with Tiffany plates and Italian dessert plates, both sets hand-painted, and glasses hand-blown by Simon Pearce. Irish Sugan chairs are covered in fabric from Soulieado. The painting of a small girl above the settle is by Gustavo Montoya, a Mexican artist.*

Left: *In the section of the bedroom that leads into the bathroom, pegs on the wall and a bench are piled with coats and hats including, at the top, a peaked straw hat brought back from China by Dana Wynter's son.*

Index

Page numbers in *italic* refer to illustrations and captions

Abercorn, James, Duke of, 14–16
Abercorn, Louisa, Duchess of, 16, 22
Abercorn, 1st Marquess of, 22
Abercorn, Sasha, Duchess of, 8, 14–23, 19
Acton, Harold, 64
Aleppo, 36
Allen, Lady, 70
Allen, Myrtle, 7, 8, 24–33, 32
Allen, Robert, 57
Andrews, Francis, 147, 148
Angoulême, Duc d', 50
Ardgillan, County Dublin, 69
Ardmore Studios, 36
Artichokes, Jerusalem *see* Jerusalem artichokes
Ashley, Laura, 42
Athboy, County Meath, 64
Avocado pear mould, 142

Baileborough Castle, County Cavan, 36
Baldwin, G. & C., 59
Ballydoyle, County Tipperary, 9, 100–6, 101–7
Ballyknockan, 128
Ballymaloe, County Cork, 8, 24–33, 25, 28, 30–3
Ballynabrocky, County Wicklow, 128–34, 129–35
Ballynacourty, County Limerick, 136–43, 137–43
Barons Court, County Tyrone, 12, 14–23, 15–23
Barry, James, 148, 148
Bass:
    Alice B. Toklas' bass, 44

Bateman, Peter, 47
Beaton, Cecil, 78, 80
Bedford, 4th Duke of, 147
Behan, John, 91, 93
Beirut, 36
Beit family, 64
Belgard Castle, 99
Berard, Christian, 78
Berenson, Bernard, 78
Berry, John, 97
Betjeman, Sir John, 78
Birr Castle, County Offaly, 9, 118–27, 119–27
Biscuits:
    Cornflake biscuits, 106
    Treacle biscuits, 150
Bisgrove, Richard, 105
Bishopscourt, County Kildare, 98
Blackberries:
    Emily's pudding, 99
Blackcurrant pudding, 143
Bokhara, 78
Book of Kells, 144
Booker, 71
Bowen, Elizabeth, 126
Boyle, Katie, 98
Brack, Wicklow, 157
Brandon, Canon, 94
Bratby, John, 78
Bray, 36, 42
Bread:
    Brown bread ice cream, 22–3
Breffny, Brian de, 11
Broghill, Lord, 26, 28
Brooke, Lady Mabel, 96
Brown bread ice cream, 22–3
Browne, Jane, 138, 141
Brownies, Wicklow, 157
Brunschwig & Fils, 55
Burke, Edmund, 148, 148
Burlington, Lord, 151
Butler, Bishop, 151
Buttevant, 71

Byrne, Eileen, 68–70, 72
Byrne, W.H., 42, 43

Caher, Lady, 150
Cahirmee horse fair, 100
Cakes:
    Gingerbread, 150
Cantrell and Cochrane, 34
Carew, Lord, 94
Carolan, 110
Carrageen:
    Chocolate carrageen, 32–3
Carrier, Robert, 28
Carrots:
    Parsnip and carrot soup, 92
Castletown House, County Kildare, 38, 98
Celbridge Lodge, County Kildare, 94–9, 95–9
'Champagne', elderflower, 133
Champagne Charlie, 87
Chanel, Coco, 48
Chanterelles, 133–4, 134
    Chanterelles à la crème, 134
Charles I, King of England, 28, 63
Charles II, King of England, 62, 110
Cheese:
    Dublin Bay prawns and eggs, 86
    Dunsany Gnocchi, 65
Cherries, rum, 117
Chicken:
    Chicken pie Massachusetts, 30–2
    Jedjad imer (honeyed chicken), 22
    Pollo alla cacciatore con pomodori, 142–3
Childers, Erskine, 40
Chippendale, Thomas, 18, 125

Chocolate:
    Chocolate carrageen, 32–3
    Chocolate fudge, 116–17
    Chocolate mousse, 57
    Rum cherries, 117
    Truffles, 117
    Wicklow brownies, 157
Chuff the Dwarf, 26, 29
Churchtown, County Cork, 100
Civic Institute, 64
Clancy, Stephen, 136
Clare, Lady, 150
Clashgannif House, County Cork, 100
Clonalis, County Roscommon, 7, 9, 108–17, 109–17
Cobbe, Bishop, 82
Coca Cola, 36
Cochrane, Admiral Lord, 34
Cochrane, Alfred, 7, 8, 34–44
Cochrane, Sir Ernest, 34, 36
Cochrane, Sir Henry, 34, 36
Cochrane, Sir Stanley, 34, 36
Cockrell, Pepys, 110
Coeur à la crème with raspberry sauce, 56
Comeragh Mountains, 100
Connaught, Duke of, 36
Connolly, Sybil, 46–59, 52
Conolly, Captain, 75
Conolly, Lady Louisa, 150
Conolly, Squire, 150
Conolly, Thomas, 96
Conolly-Carew family, 98
Cordon Bleu school, 52–4
Corke Lodge, County Wicklow, 34–44, 35–42
Corker, Colonel, 29
Cornflake biscuits, 106
Coster, Anne Vallayer, 55

Cotbrook river, 84
Cream cheese:
    Coeur à la crème with raspberry sauce, 56
Cromer, William, 96
Cromwell, Oliver, 28, 60, 62
Cross of Cong, 110, 114, 116
Crowley, Nicholas, 140
Crowthers of London, 84, 84
Curley, Mr, 154

Dargan, William, 36
De Freyne, Lord, 36
De Marsillac, Maria Alice, 41
De Morgan, William, 76, 79
Dearle, 76, 80
Decies family, 75
Deer Society, 18
Delaney, Mrs, 55, 58
Denny, Lady, 150
Dickens, Charles, 34
Dickinson, Emily, 80
Djouce Mountains, 156
Dodder river, 82
Doneraile, 71
Donoghmore, Lady, 52
Donovan, James, 140, 142
Dromoland Castle, County Clare, 70
Dublin, 36
    71 Merrion Square, 46–59, 47–59
Dublin Bay prawns and eggs, 86
Dublin Institute of Technology, 121
Dunne, Annie, 72
Dunsany, 1st Baron, 62, 64
Dunsany, 19th Baron, 41, 60–2, 64
Dunsany, Lady, 8, 41, 60–5
Dunsany Castle, County Meath, 60–5, 61–4

Dunsany Gnocchi, 65

Eggs:
    Dublin Bay prawns and
      eggs, 86
Elderflowers:
    Elderflower 'champagne',
      133
    Gooseberry and
      elderflower syrup, 133
Elizabeth I, Queen of
    England, 147–8, *147*, 149
Emerson, Audrey, 70
Emily's pudding, 99
Engelhard, Charlie, 106
Engelhard, Jane, 106
Eugene, Prince of Savoy,
    114

Featherbed Mountains, 152
Fiji, 52
FitzGerald, Sir Edmond, 28
Fitzgerald, Geraldine, 36
Fitzgerald, Lord Henry, 150
FitzGerald family, 28
Fitzgerald family, 62
Fletcher, Lionel, 96
Florence, 60
Foster family, 29
Francis of Assisi, St, *52*
Fudge, chocolate, 116–17

Gaelic League, 111
Gaelic pheasant, 65
Galbreath, John, 106
Gale, Martin, 91, *93*
Galtee Mountains, 100, 102
Garbo, Greta, 78, *80*
Geddes, Lord, 46
George V, King of England,
    110
Georgian State Dancers, 18
Gingerbread, 150
Gladstone, William, *110*
The Glebe, County
    Donegal, 76–81, *77–81*
Glenasmole Lodge, County
    Dublin, 82–7, *83–7*
Glendalough House, 38–40,
    155, 156
Glenmacnass, County
    Wicklow, 152–7, *153–7*
Glyndebourne, 36
Gnocchi, Dunsany, 65
Gogarty, Oliver, 62
Golden Vale, 100, *104*
Gooseberries:
    Gooseberry and
      elderflower syrup, 133

Gooseberry creame, 127
Gordon, Ann, 55
Gorges family, *69*
Gowing, Lawrence, 78
Gowrie, Lord, 8, 96
Grant, Ulysses S., 111
Greaves, Derrick, 78
Green & Abbott, 76
Gregory, Lady, 62
Grierson, George, 82
Guest, Caroline, 106
Guest, Raymond, 106
Guinness, Arthur, 68
Guinness, Desmond, 8, 11,
    38, 66–75, 96
Guinness, Jasmin, *67*, 68
Guinness, Liz, 68
Guinness, Mariga, 11, 96
Guinness, Marina, 68
Guinness, Patrick, 68
Guinness, Penny, *70*, *75*
Guinness, Richard, 66–8

Ham:
    Veal and ham press,
      29–30
Hamilton, Lady Emma, 16
Hamilton, Lady Sophie, *19*
Hare, St George, 140
Harpers & Queen, 68
Harty, Sir Hamilton, 36
Healy, Michael, 91
Hely-Hutchinson, John, 148
Henn, Helen, 46
Henn, Judge, 46
Henn, William, 46
Henrietta Maria, Queen, 63
Henry VI, King of England,
    62, *64*
Hepburn, Katharine, 36
Hickey, Patrick, 91, *93*
Hicks, David, 16, 18, *19*, 22
Highfield Hall, Flintshire,
    96
Hill, Derek, 8, 64, 76–81, *80*
Hill, John, 76
Home-made toffee, 117
Honey:
    Jedjad imer (honeyed
      chicken), 22
House & Garden, 30
Hunt, John, 7
Huston, Ricky, 78
Hyde, Douglas, 114

Ice cream:
    Brown bread ice cream,
      22–3
    Champagne Charlie, 87

IRA, 82
Irish College, Rome, 62
Irish Georgian Society, 8,
    11, 70–2
Irish moss seaweed:
    Chocolate carrageen,
      32–3
Irish rice pudding, 92
Irish Tourist Board, 64
Iznik, 78

Jedjad imer (honeyed
    chicken), 22
Jerusalem artichoke soup,
    72–5
John, King of England, 66
Jordaens, Jakob, 18
Judd, Charlie, 8
Judd, June, 8, 82–7

Keane, Molly, 9, 10–14, 68
Kearns, Martin, 130
Kearns, Sheila, 130
Keenan, John, 42
Keene, Henry, *151*
Keery, Knights of, 28
Kilkenny Castle, 64
Kindel company, *72*
King's Own Scottish
    Borderers, 65
Knights of Kerry, 28
Knights of Malta, 64
Knockmealdown
    Mountains, 100
Kokoschka, Oskar, 78, *79*

Lady Moyne's lobster
    bisque, 80
Lamb:
    Roast lamb, 116
Lancaster, Osbert, 78
Landseer, Sir Edwin, 16, *17*,
    22
Langley, Batty, *67*
Lastman, Pieter, *148*
Lauderdale, Lady, 98
Laurel Park Opera House, 36
Lavery, Sir John, 95
Lawrence, Sir Thomas, 16,
    22
Le Broquay, Louis, *33*
Leclerc, *70*
Leigh-Fermor, Patrick, 78
Leinster, 62
Leinster, Duke of, 150
Leixlip Castle, County
    Kildare, 8, 66–75, *67–75*,
    96

Lemon:
    Sharp lemon mousse, 75
Leyden, Paddy, 136
Leyla's Turkish soup, 80
Lichfield, Caroline, 24
Lichfield, Myra, 24
Lichfield family, 29
Liffey, river, 66
Lismore, 48
Lloyd, 46
Lobster:
    Lady Moyne's lobster
      bisque, 80
Lough Tay, *135*
Louis XIV, King of France,
    110
Lumley, Hugh, 29

McDonnell, Peggy, 8,
    88–92, *91*
McDonnell, Richard, 149
McDowell, Henry, 8, 94–9
McDowell, Joan, 94–6, 99
McGillycuddy family, 98
McIlhenny, Henry, 78
McNulty, Mrs Alfred P., 71
McShain, John, 106
Madden, Samuel, 148, *148*
Madigan, Margaret, 141
Magan, Georgina Augusta,
    34, 36, 38
Mahon, Tommy, 82
al Maktoum, Sheikh
    Mohammed, 106
Malahide Castle, *70*
Malcomson, Anthony, 121
Manorbier Castle,
    Pembrokeshire, 60
Margaret, Princess of Hesse
    and the Rhine, 46
Marie-Antoinette, Queen of
    France, 16
Martex, *51*
Matisse, Henri, 44
Maude family, *99*
Maxwell brothers, 84
Melba, Dame Nellie, 16, 36
Menuhin, Yehudi, 78
Meringue:
    Mona Harrison Williams'
      vacherin, 82
Merrion Square, Dublin,
    46–59, *47–59*
Messel, Oliver, *124*
Middleditch, Edward, 78
Miles, Sarah, 98
Milford Haven, 60
Miller, William, 138
Mitford family, 72

Mona Harrison Williams'
    vacherin, 82
Montegufoni, 78
Montoya, Gustavo, *157*
Moore, George, 62
Morris, William, 76, *79*, *80*
Morrison, J. W., *148*
Mott, George, 11
Mount Sorrel, *130*
Mountbatten, Lord, 18
Mountcashel, County
    Clare, 138
Mountjoy, Lord, 28
Mousses:
    Chocolate mousse, 57
    Sharp lemon mousse, 75
Moyne, Lady, 80
Mulcahy, Jack, 106
Multiple Sclerosis Society,
    64
Mushrooms:
    Chicken pie
      Massachusetts, 30–2

Napolean I, Emperor, 100,
    106
Napoleonic wars, 10
Nara, 78
National Museum, Dublin,
    28, 110
Nectarines glacées, 44
Newbridge, Donasbate, *73*
Niarchos, Maria, 106
Niarchos, Stavros, 106
Normans, 62
North of Ireland Public
    Records Office, 121

O'Brien, Dermot, 100
O'Brien, Jacqueline, 9,
    100–6
O'Brien, Vincent, 100–4,
    103, *105*–6
O'Connell, Daniel, *110*
O'Conor, Rev. Charles,
    108, 114, *116*
O'Conor, Father Charles,
    114
O'Conor, Charles, of
    Ballinagare, 111
O'Conor, Charles, of
    Mount Allen, 111
O'Conor, Charles, of New
    York, 111
O'Conor, Denis, 111
O'Conor, Felim, *110*
O'Conor family, 111–16, *111*
O'Conor Don, Charles
    Owen, 111, *113*

O'Conor Don, Owen, 111
O'Conor-Nash, Gertrude, 108
O'Conor-Nash, Letitia, 114
O'Conor-Nash, Marguerite, 9, 108–17
O'Conor-Nash, Pyers, 108
Ohio, 71
O'Neill, Hugh, Earl of Tyrone, 28
Orange:
    Champagne Charlie, 87
Order of St Lazarus of Jerusalem, 64
O'Rourke, Bishop Thaddeus, 112, 114
O'Toole, Luke, 156
Oyster soup, 127

Palermo, 38
Palladio, Andrea, 151
Paradise Hall, County Clare, 46
Parsnip and carrot soup, 92
Parsons, Sir Charles, 121
Parsons, Dorothy, 122, 127
Pasmore, Victor, 78, 79
Peaches:
    Emily's pudding, 99
    Peaches glacées, 44
Pearce, Sir Edward Lovett, 70
Pearce, Philip, 91
Pearce, Simon, 91, 93, 157
Pearce, Stephen, 57, 93
Pheasant:
    Gaelic pheasant, 65
    'The Pheasantry', 13
Picasso, Claude, 78
Picasso, Pablo, 7, 44, 78, 81
Picasso, Paloma, 78
Pickering Forest, 96
Picton Castle, Pembrokeshire, 60
Pies:
    Chicken pie Massachusetts, 30–2
    Salmon koulibiac, 54
Plunket, Aileen, 42
Plunkett, Lady Beatrice, 62
Plunkett, Beatrice, 60

Plunkett, Eddie, 41
Plunkett, Sir Horace, 62
Plunkett, Sir Oliver, 62
Plunkett family, 62
Pollo alla cacciatore con pomodori, 142–3
Pommes Duchesse, 22
Ponte a Mensola, 78
Poole, Shona Crawford, 57
Pot-pourri, 59
Potatotes:
    Pommes Duchesse, 22
Prawns:
    Dublin Bay prawns and eggs, 86
    Prawns en cocotte Americaine, 21
Price, Archbishop Arthur, 66–8
Price, Joe, 72
Provost's House, Trinity College, Dublin, 9, 144–50, 145–51
Pushkin, Alexander, 8

Rackham, Arthur, 62
Rapier, Alan, 104
Rapier, Nora, 104
Raspberries:
    Coeur à la crème with raspberry sauce, 56
Ravenna, 78
Redesdale, Lady, 75
Rice pudding, Irish, 92
Richardson, Lionel, 104
Roast lamb, 116
Robertson, Daniel, 40
Rock of Cashel, 104
Rome, 36, 62
Rorrimer, James, 7
Roses, Pot-pourri, 59
Rosse, Alice, Countess of, 127
Rosse, Alison, Countess of, 9, 118–27, 121, 124
Rosse, Brendan, Earl of, 9, 124
Rosse, Cassandra, Countess of, 127
Rosse, 2nd Earl of, 125
Rosse, Mary, Countess of, 9, 121, 122, 124, 124

Rum cherries, 117
Russell, A.E., 62
Rutzen, Baron de, 60
Ryan, Thomas, 140
Rye water, 66

Sadler, William, 95
Sadler family, 100
Salmon, Provost, 148
Salmon koulibiac, 54
Samarkand, 78
Sangster, Robert, 106
Sant, James, 98
Sauce, raspberry, 56
Schiaparelli, Elsa, 78
Scones, 33
Scott, Patrick, 9, 91, 128–34, 132, 135
Seasickness remedy, 127
Shackleton, Arthur, 105
Shanagarry pottery, 91
Shannon, river, 137
Sharp lemon mousse, 75
Shaw, George Bernard, 62
Shaw, Giles, 96
Shaw, Sarah Eliza, 96
Shiel, James, 34
Shortt, Annie, 122
Simpson, Helen, 24, 29
Simpson, Jim, 24
Simpson, Joan, 24, 29
Simpson, Marion, 24, 28
Simpson, Priscilla, 24, 29
Sitwell, Osbert, 78
Slade Brook river, 84
Slieve Bloom hills, 126
Smyth, John, 151
Soane, Sir John, 16
Society for the Prevention of Cruelty to Animals, 64, 99
Sotheby's, 41, 96
Soups:
    Jerusalem artichoke soup, 72–5
    Lady Moyne's lobster bisque, 80
    Leyla's Turkish soup, 80
    Oyster soup, 127
    Parsnip and carrot soup, 92

Sperrin Mountains, 14
Spry, Constance, 59
Stacpoole, Frederick, 140–1
Stacpoole, George, 9, 136–43
Stacpoole, Hassard, 140
Stacpoole, James, 138
Stacpoole, Michelina, 9, 136, 141
Stacpoole, Richard John, 139, 140
Stacpoole, Sebastian, 140
Stein, Gertrude, 43
Stephens, James, 62
Steuart, George, 16
Stillorgan, County Dublin, 70
Straffan, County Kildare, 88–92, 89–93
Suir, River, 13
The Sunday Times, 28
Sutherland, Graham, 60
Swiss Cottage, 13

Taubman, Mr and Mrs Alfred, 41
Tiffany, 47, 58, 78, 157
The Times, 57
Timmons, Mrs, 96
Toffee, home-made, 117
Toklas, Alice B., 7, 43–4
Tomato:
    Pollo alla cacciatore con pomodori, 142–3
Toms, Carl, 119
Treacle biscuits, 150
Trinity College, Dublin, 9, 144–50, 145–51
Truffles, 117
Turlough Mor O'Connor, high king of Ireland, 110, 114
Tyburn, 62

United States of America, 71
Ussher, James, 148

Vacherin:
    Mona Harrison Williams' vacherin, 82

Van Dyck, Sir Anthony, 63
Veal and ham press, 29–30
Vernet, school of, 87
Versailles, 16
Victoria, Queen of England, 34, 98
Vikings, 62
Villafranca, Princess of, 43
Voltaire, 127

Wade, General, 151
Wales, 60
Wall brothers, 147
Watts, Gerry, 9
Watts, Mai, 90
Watts, Mrs William, 144–50
Waugh, Evelyn, 70
Wells, H.G., 62
Wexford Opera Festival, 46
Weygand, Madame, 42–3
Wheatley, Francis, 55
Whipple Museum, Cambridge, 121
Whitechurch Stud, County Kildare, 8, 88–92, 89–93
Wicklow brack, 157
Wicklow brownies, 157
William III, King of England, 29
Williams, Mona Harrison, 81
Windlesham, Lord, 36
Wingate-Saul, Nicola, 71
Wood, John A., 102
Woodbrook, County Wicklow, 34, 36, 42
The Workshops of the Blind, 90
Wynter, Dana, 9, 152–7, 155

Yasawa Islands, 52
Yeats, Jack B., 8, 65
Yeats, W.B., 62
Yoghurt:
    Emily's pudding, 99
    Leyla's Turkish soup, 80

Zoffany, Johann, 64